Golden Spike National Historic Site
Geologic Resource Evaluation Report

Natural Resource Report NPS/NRPC/GRD/NRR—2006/010

Geologic Resources Division
Natural Resource Program Center
P.O. Box 25287
Denver, Colorado 80225

July 2006

U.S. Department of the Interior
Washington, D.C.

The Natural Resource Publication series addresses natural resource topics that are of interest and applicability to a broad readership in the National Park Service and to others in the management of natural resources, including the scientific community, the public, and the NPS conservation and environmental constituencies. Manuscripts are peer-reviewed to ensure that the information is scientifically credible, technically accurate, appropriately written for the intended audience, and is designed and published in a professional manner.

Natural Resource Reports are the designated medium for disseminating high priority, current natural resource management information with managerial application. The series targets a general, diverse audience, and may contain NPS policy considerations or address sensitive issues of management applicability. Examples of the diverse array of reports published in this series include vital signs monitoring plans; "how to" resource management papers; proceedings of resource management workshops or conferences; annual reports of resource programs or divisions of the Natural Resource Program Center; resource action plans; fact sheets; and regularly-published newsletters.

Views and conclusions in this report are those of the authors and do not necessarily reflect policies of the National Park Service. Mention of trade names or commercial products does not constitute endorsement or recommendation for use by the National Park Service.

Printed copies of reports in these series may be produced in a limited quantity and they are only available as long as the supply lasts. This report is also available from the Geologic Resource Evaluation Program website (http://www2.nature.nps.gov/geology/inventory/gre_publications) on the internet, or by sending a request to the address on the back cover. Please cite this publication as:

NPS D-215, July 2006

Table of Contents

List of Figures

Executive Summary

This report has been developed to accompany the digital geologic map produced by Geologic Resource Evaluation staff for Golden Spike National Historic Site in Utah. It contains information relevant to resource management and scientific research.

Knowing the geology of Golden Spike National Historic Site enhances one's understanding of the unique relationship between geology and the environment. Geology provides the foundation of the entire ecosystem. Surface exposures in Golden Spike consist primarily of rocks from the Devonian, Mississippian, Pennsylvanian, Permian, and Tertiary ages. Vast unconsolidated Quaternary deposits overlay these units. Detailed geologic information helps determine the history of Golden Spike National Historic Site and helps managers preserve its present resources.

Geologic processes initiate complex responses that give rise to rock formation, surface and subsurface fluid movement, soils, and mountain formation. These processes produce a landscape that influences patterns of human use. Preserving the historic context at Golden Spike inspires wonder in visitors to the park, imparting geologic knowledge to these same visitors is sure to enhance their experience.

The Promontory Mountains, a small part of the dramatic Basin and Range physiographic province, provided the backdrop for the joining of the Central Pacific and Union Pacific railroads at Golden Spike 1869. This historic site defined by its geology, attracted over 45,888 visitors in 2002. Visitors were impressed by the historic engineering marvels made necessary by the geologic setting. The history of the area results from regional geology and reflects the human struggle to manipulate the landscape. The number of visitors attracted to this unique site are placing increasing demands on the resources available at the park.

Golden Spike National Historic Site hosts some of the most complete relics of the grand era of railroad building. The interplay of geology, water, tectonic forces, and climate posed a great challenge for railroad engineers. Some of the principal geologic issues and concerns pertain to protecting the historic landscape. Humans have modified the landscape surrounding Golden Spike and, consequently, have modified the base geologic system. This system is dynamic and capable of noticeable change within a human life span (less than a century) even without human alterations.

The following features, issues, and processes were identified as having the most geological importance and the highest level of management significance at the historic site:

- Flooding, Erosion, and Gullying. Arid environments are especially susceptible to erosion during flooding because of lack of stabilizing plant growth and the relatively frequent occurrence of intense seasonal rainstorms. Intense storms produce runoff that dramatically alters the landscape and creates new hazard areas in the process. Cut and fill for railroad construction as well as for road and trail construction affect the stability of the slopes. Rockfalls and slope failures could occur almost anywhere along the roads and trails of Golden Spike National Historic Site.

- Seismicity and Mining Activity. The area around Golden Spike National Historic Site is seismically active. Impacts from seismicity and ground shaking from detonation of explosive in nearby mines have the potential to damage historic features and facilities at Golden Spike.

- Disturbed Lands. Borrow pits, gravel pits, animal grazing, housing construction, and other outside development adjacent to park lands impact the soil, vegetation, and the viewshed of the site. Park management may wish to consider establishing cooperative relationships with the parties involved in order to remediate and restore disturbed areas.

- Historic Landscape and Present Condition. Geology influenced the decisions of the railroad construction engineers, with challenges to constructing the transcontinental railroad that are still visible at Golden Spike. Golden Spike National Historic Site is charged with preserving and restoring the historic landscape from 1869. Fighting the natural, geological processes of erosion and weathering is essential to maintain the historic landscape.

Other geologic management issues at the Golden Spike National Historic Site include: protecting the paleontological potential of the area; contending with the effects of wind erosion and deposition, landslides and slope processes, faulting and deformation processes, possible volcanism; and managing cave resources. These are discussed in more detail in the Geologic Issues section of this report.

The variety of rock types together with the geologic processes of uplift and erosion have created the topographic landscape seen today. Understanding these features and processes allows resource managers to assess potential hazards and to protect the environment, the historic context, and especially park visitors.

The Formation Properties section details the different geologic units present on the digital geologic map of Golden Spike National Historic Site and potential resources, concerns, and issues associated with each.

Introduction

The following section briefly describes the regional geologic setting and the National Park Service Geologic Resource Evaluation program.

Purpose of the Geologic Resource Evaluation Program

Geologic features and processes serve as the foundation of park ecosystems and an understanding of geologic resources yields important information for park decision making. The National Park Service (NPS) Natural Resource Challenge, an action plan to advance the management and protection of park resources, has focused efforts to inventory the natural resources of parks. Ultimately, the inventory and monitoring of natural resources will become integral parts of park planning, operations and maintenance, visitor protection, and interpretation.

The Geologic Resource Evaluation (GRE) Program, which the NPS Geologic Resources Division administers, carries out the geologic component of the inventory. Staff associated with other programs within the Geologic Resources Division (e.g., the abandoned mine land, cave, coastal, disturbed lands restoration, minerals management, and paleontology programs) provide expertise to the GRE effort. The goal of the GRE Program is to provide each of the identified 270 "natural area" parks with a digital geologic map, a geologic resource evaluation report, and a geologic bibliography. Each product is a tool to support the stewardship of park resources and is designed to be user friendly to non-geoscientists.

GRE teams hold scoping meetings at parks to review available data on the geology of a particular park and to discuss specific geologic issues affecting the park. Park staff are afforded the opportunity to meet with park geology experts during these meetings. Scoping meetings are usually held for individual parks although some address an entire Vital Signs Monitoring Network.

Bedrock and surficial geologic maps and information provide the foundation for studies of groundwater, geomorphology, soils, and environmental hazards. Geologic maps describe the underlying physical framework of many natural systems and are an integral component of the physical inventories stipulated by the NPS in its Natural Resources Inventory and Monitoring Guideline (NPS- 75) and the 1997 NPS Strategic Plan. The NPS GRE is a cooperative implementation of a systematic, comprehensive inventory of the geologic resources in National Park System units by the Geologic Resources Division; the Inventory, Monitoring, and Evaluation Office of the Natural Resource Program Center; the U.S. Geological Survey; and state geological surveys.

For additional information regarding the content of this report, please refer to the Geologic Resources Division of the National Park Service, located in Denver, Colorado. Up- to- date contact information is available on the GRE website (http://www2.nature.nps.gov/geology/inventory/).

Geologic Setting

On May 10, 1869, "Done," a single telegraphed word signaling to the nation the completion of the first transcontinental railroad was sent from Promontory Summit some 80 km (50 miles) northwest of Ogden, Utah, in Box Elder County. The Central Pacific and Union Pacific railroads met here amidst much celebration and showcasing the engineering marvels. Completion of the transcontinental railroad united the country with high- speed rail access from the east coast to the west coast with a single golden spike made from California gold and driven by Leland Stanford, president of the Central Pacific Railroad, and others. The spike was engraved with the words, "May God continue the unity of our Country as this Railroad unites the two great Oceans of the world." This spike now resides at Stanford University.

It was the dawn of a new era in the American West. Prior to completion of the railroad, the journey was either a long stagecoach ride from end- of- rail to the west coast or an even longer sailing trip around the tip of South America. Both options were dangerous and tedious, usually taking several months. The new, 4- day route was envisioned as a means to move mail, supplies, and people immigrating to the west. For more detailed information on the history of the railroad's construction and western expansion, refer to the following informational website: http://www.outdoorplaces.com/Destination/USNP/utgo lspi/

Golden Spike was designated as a National Historic Site in nonfederal ownership on April 2, 1957. The mission of the site is to preserve the historical context that surrounded the completion of the first transcontinental railroad across the United States and to illustrate the social, economic, and political impacts of the railroad on the growth and westward development. On July 30, 1965, an act of congress authorized Golden Spike for federal ownership and administration.

Some 690 miles east of Sacramento and 1,087 miles west of Omaha, the 2,735 acres of Golden Spike National Historic Site lie in the extreme northeastern part of the Great Basin, a subdivision of the Basin and Range Physiographic province. The province is characterized by long, linear ranges separated by parallel valleys. The valleys are bounded by a series of normal faults (see glossary) along which extensional deformation occurred. Elevations range from 1,311 to 1,494 m (4,300 to 4,900 ft) above sea level (figure 1)

There are many parallel ranges throughout the region that developed as a result of extensional tectonics pulling the crust apart in a roughly east- west oriented pattern. The Cedar, Oquirrh, and Promontory ranges to the west of the Wasatch Range, and the Cricket Mountains, Pavant, and Confusion ranges to the south and southwest are examples of parallel ranges. Basins including the Tule, Snake, and Great Salt Lake valleys surrounding Golden Spike, as well as Cedar and Little valleys, and Sevier Basin to the southwest are typical examples of the fault bound basins in the province.

The Wasatch Mountain Range forms the sharp eastern boundary of the Basin and Range separating it from the Middle Rocky Mountain physiographic province. The Wasatch Range is an uplifted crustal block that extends approximately 200 km (125 mi) from Malad City, ID, south to Nephi, UT. The range is 13 to 26 km (8 to 16 mi) wide and is bounded dramatically on the western side by the prominent scarp of the seismically active Wasatch fault. The scarp, referred to as the Wasatch Front, rises dramatically up to 2,134 m (7,000 ft) from the valley floor below.

A fundamental human compulsion to know the world is stimulated by the landscape at Golden Spike National Historic Site (De Courten 1994). Preservation of this environment is facilitated by natural resource management and increased understanding of the underlying geologic processes affecting the trails and other visitor facilities.

The Joining of Two Tracks

The meeting of the Union Pacific and the Central Pacific Railroads was more than a joining of rails; it changed the course of western expansion and culture forever. For a brief moment, it changed the local setting around Promontory, Utah, as well. Crews of the Union Pacific, 8,000 to 10,000 Irish, German, and Italian immigrants, had pushed west from Omaha, Nebraska, while laborers including over 10,000 Chinese built the line east from Sacramento, California (Kraus 1969). These workers were among many others who helped link the east with the west. Promontory continued to be a town of tents and rudimentary shacks for several weeks after the joining ceremony. Land speculators, petty merchants, saloon keepers, gamblers, and prostitutes who had followed these so- called tent cities stayed only as long as there were workers to entice and money to be made. Promontory, Utah, never became the site of a permanent town (figure 2) perhaps due to its isolated location.

President Abraham Lincoln signed the Pacific Railways Act in 1862. Federal legislation at the time encouraged building railroads with subsidies. Companies building tracks received loans of $16,000, $32,000, and $48,000 for building each mile of track across the plains, the Great Basin, and the mountains, respectively. Railroad companies also received 10 alternate sections of land on each side of the railroad right- of- way (Gwynn 2002). As a result of this policy, railroad builders were reluctant to

stop construction, and the crews built several miles of track parallel to each other before Congress acted to set the meeting point at Promontory. The ceremony held on May 10, 1869, has various witness accounts with many discrepancies; however, a general description is as follows:

"Union Pacific's No. 119 and Central Pacific's "Jupiter" engines lined up facing each other on the tracks, separated only by the width of one rail (figure 3). Leland Stanford, one of the "Big Four" of the Central Pacific, had brought four ceremonial spikes. The famed "Golden Spike" was presented by David Hewes, a San Francisco construction magnate. It was engraved with the names of the Central Pacific directors, special sentiments appropriate to the occasion, and, on the head, the notation "the Last Spike." A second golden spike was presented by the San Francisco News Letter. A silver spike was Nevada's contribution, and a spike blended of iron, silver, and gold represented Arizona. These spikes were dropped into a pre- bored laurelwood tie during the ceremony. No spike represented Utah, and Mormon Church leaders were conspicuous by their absence (Ketterson 1969).

At 12:47 P.M. the actual last spike- - an ordinary iron spike- - was driven into a regular tie. Both spike and sledge were wired to send the sound of the strikes over the wire to the nation" (Blake).

The enthusiasm for the event soon faded. In 1901 the Central Pacific steam engine "Jupiter" was scrapped for iron and other materials. The Union Pacific's No. 119 was scrapped 2 years later. The 1903- 04 rail line construction of the Lucin Cutoff diverted most of the traffic from Promontory's "Old Line" across Great Salt Lake (Gwynn 2002). Only the "Last Spike" remained - preserved at Stanford University in Palo Alto, California.

During World War II in 1942, the old rails over the 76 km (123 mi) Promontory Summit rail line were salvaged in ceremonies marking the "Undriving of the Golden Spike." Tourists and relic hunters picked over the area for ties and other mementos. The area seemed destined for quiet obscurity (Mann 1969).

However, a small memorial marker of the "Last Spike" had been placed along the right- of- way in 1943; and in the years following World War II, local residents began observing the event. In the 1948 reenactment of the driving of the last spike, miniature locomotives were produced and distributed by the Southern Pacific Railroad Co.

In 1951 a monument to the event was dedicated and placed in front of the Union Station in Ogden, Utah. After a series of legislative actions, Golden Spike National Historic Site was established; and in 1965 Weber County extended the highway from 12th Street to Promontory, which made access to the site easier (Blake).

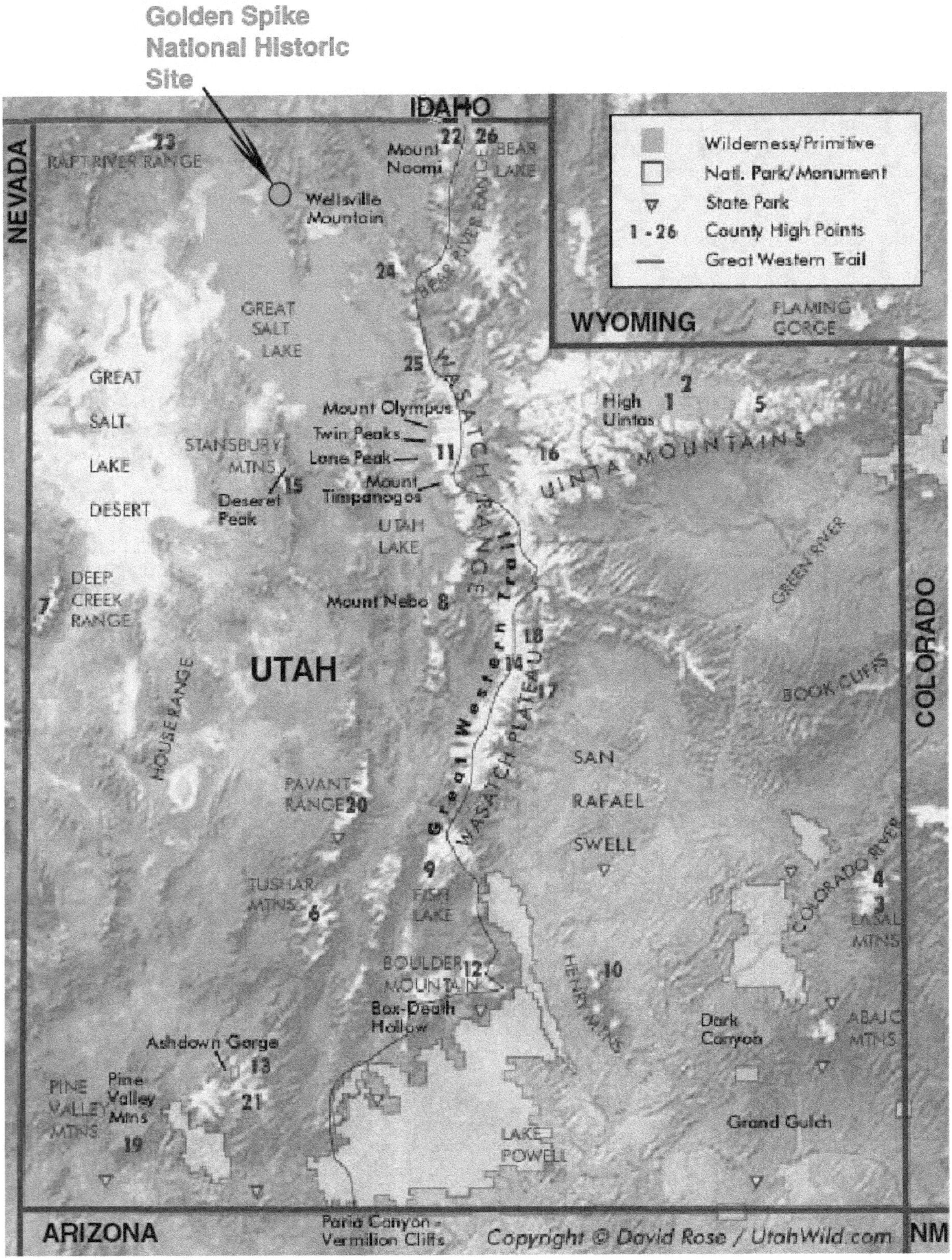

Figure 1. Map of the physiographic features surrounding Golden Spike National Historic Site. Note the location of Golden Spike and the Wasatch Range to the east. West of the Wasatch Range the mountains are arranged in roughly parallel, linear chains. Adapted from image by David Rose from www.UtahWild.com.

Figure 2. The shanty town development at Promontory, Utah. Photograph from A.J. Russell. This and other Russell photographs are available at http://www.uprr.com/aboutup/photos/ajrussellstereo/ (accessed April 4, 2004)

Figure 3. The joining of the rails ceremony at Promontory, Utah. The two steam engines, "No. 119" and "Jupiter," face off while the four final spikes are driven. Photograph from A.J. Russell.

Geologic Issues

A Geologic Resource Evaluation scoping session was held for Golden Spike National Historic Site, June 15- 16, 1999, to discuss geologic resources, to address the status of geologic mapping, and to assess resource management issues and needs. The following section synthesizes the scoping results, in particular, those issues that may require attention from resource managers.

Introduction

Issues in this section are identified in relative order of resource management significance with the most critical listed first. Potential research projects and topics of scientific interest are presented at the end of this section.

Flooding, Erosion, and Gullying

Floods have the potential to create hazards in much of the Golden Spike area. Intense seasonal thunderstorms combine with a scarcity of stabilizing vegetation on slopes creating a situation in which flooding can send torrents of water and debris down grades, destroying trails, roads, and other park facilities. In addition to threatening park infrastructure flash floods are a visitor safety concern.

Several Holocene alluvial fans mapped along both sides of the North Promontory Mountains have been active since the deposition of Bonneville lacustrine deposits. All are probable sites for future alluviation, including debris flows and deposition during floods. Narrow canyons upslope from the fans are also potential sites for powerful floods and debris flows.

Gullying occurs in many areas underlain by unconsolidated to moderately consolidated materials. The uplands, areas of intensive agriculture east of the North Promontory Mountains, show especially pronounced gullying. The fine- grained Miocene, Pliocene, and Quaternary materials in the Sunset Pass quadrangle are highly susceptible to erosion following the destruction of natural ground cover by overgrazing and ground tilling.

Inventory, Monitoring, and/or Research Needs for Flooding, Erosion, and Gullying

- Study the flood history of deposition behind culverts and filled grades and compare the findings with the historic climate records. This will lead to a better understanding of erosion and the stability of culverts and trestles.
- Study, describe, map, and monitor flood deposits behind railroad embankments.

Seismicity and Mining Activity

The Basin and Range is a seismically active area. Small scale earthquakes occur in Nevada and Utah almost daily. Most of these quakes are too small to be detected without a seismometer. The region from Hansel Valley east to the Wasatch Mountains has experienced considerable historic seismic activity, including magnitude 6 and larger events in Hansel Valley in 1909 and 1934 (figure 4). The Wasatch Front east of Golden Spike is considered "due" for a major earthquake.

No historical earthquakes associated with surface rupture faulting have occurred along the Wasatch fault zone during at least the past 133 years. However, the recurrence interval, or time between major seismic events, for the entire Wasatch fault zone may be 50 to 430 years (Swan et al. 1980).

Golden Spike National Historic Site is located near several active mines that use blasting to extract ore, coal, and other mineral resources. These blasts produce seismic waves that propagate through the earth and produce significant ground shaking.

The historic landscape is a major reason that the Golden Spike area was set aside for preservation and protection. The effect of ground shaking on local geomorphology is a significant resource management issue because of the potential for its occurrence in the area as a result of natural or manmade causes.

No fault scarps or faults cutting upper Pleistocene deposits were discovered during miscellaneous 1980's field investigations surrounding Golden Spike. The youngest faults cut the oldest alluvial fan deposits of Pliocene and lower Pleistocene age, but do not cut upper Pleistocene deposits, and are probably no younger than middle Pleistocene in age. However, several Quaternary and historic surface ruptures have been documented within a short distance of the Sunset Pass area, and Holocene alluvium or talus may have covered similar young scarps in the Sunset Pass quadrangle. The western flank of the North Promontory Mountains has a particularly abrupt topographic expression. Jordan (1985) and Robison and McCalpin (1987) mapped normal faults, cutting Pleistocene alluvial fan deposits in one area and Lake Bonneville deposits in another north of the Sunset Pass quadrangle along the mountain front (see figure 4).

The regional history of seismic activity and evidence for Quaternary faults in Hansel Valley raise the possibility of moderate to large earthquakes in the Sunset Pass quadrangle and, by extension, the Golden Spike area. The Wasatch fault zone and related faults 50- km (30 mi) to the east project westward at moderate angles, presenting a potential for a major seismic event that could strongly shake the Golden Spike region. In addition to hazards from ground shaking and surface rupture, lateral spreads and localized liquefaction could result from a major earthquake.

Inventory, Monitoring, and/or Research Needs for Seismicity and Mining Activity

- Perform a comprehensive study of the faulting and seismic processes active at Golden Spike National Historic Site, taking into account rock formations, slope aspects, and location and likelihood of instability.

- Evaluate railroad cuts on Golden Spike. The slopes of these areas are likely to fail in a moderate to large seismic event. Providing safe trails and other visitor access along steep hillsides and/or cuts beneath rockfall- prone areas requires careful planning.

- Monitor seismic activity in the Golden Spike area by cooperating with local agencies including the USGS and Utah Geological Survey.

- Study the effects on the historic features at Golden Spike of nearby mining practices including blasting. Determine how this relates to natural seismicity in the area.

- Perform an exhaustive study of seismically active faults in close proximity to the Golden Spike area including the mapping of small scale faults and shear fractures.

Landslides and Other Slope Processes

Landslides, slumps, and other forms of slope failure are common for geologic units that are not necessarily associated with cliffs. Unconsolidated alluvial deposits are especially vulnerable to failure when exposed on a slope. A few isolated landslides are present within lacustrine deposits as well as in Miocene deposits in the northwest corner of the Golden Spike region. The slumps within lacustrine materials in the east- central part of the area involve thick lacustrine gravel deposits that probably were built northward by shoreline processes with the gravels overlapping finer grained sediments. These features create steep, unstable slopes where slides are likely to continue.

Torrential rains that produce flash flooding at Golden Spike also act on slopes lacking stabilizing plant and tree roots by saturating and mobilizing the rock and soil producing huge slumps, mudslides, or debris flows.

Many trails in the park follow original railroad grades and lead visitors through interesting scenery. These trails may be at risk for rockfall and landslides. The rock overhead is prone to fall where the railroad bed passes through cuts in limestone potentially exposing hikers to a hazardous situation.

Inventory, Monitoring, and/or Research Needs for Landslides and Other Slope Processes

- Perform a comprehensive study of the erosion and weathering processes active at Golden Spike National Historic Site. Take into account the different rock formations versus slope aspects, location and stability.

- Create a rockfall susceptibility map using rock unit versus slope aspect in a Geographic Information System (GIS). Use the map to aid in planning future NPS developments and evaluating current resource management practices regarding trails, buildings, and recreational use areas.

- Monitor rockfall potential in the railroad cuts; relate to slope and loose rock deposits.

- Inventory and monitor debris flow potential near picnic areas; relate to slope and loose rock deposits.

- Inventory flash flood susceptible areas; relate to climate and confluence areas.

- Perform trail stability studies and determine which trails are most at risk and in need of further stabilization.

- Monitor the location of facilities in relation to fractures and potential for sloughing. Evaluate these areas for future risks.

Disturbed Lands

There are several human- made scars on the landscape at Golden Spike which have little or nothing to do with the historical relevancy of the area. These include borrow pits for sand and gravel, areas for animal grazing, development adjacent to NPS land, and nearby private gravel pits such as the Adams Ranch gravel operation. These situations may require reclamation to fulfill the goal of preserving and restoring the historical landscape that accompanied completion of the first transcontinental railroad.

Inventory, Monitoring, and/or Research Needs for Disturbed Lands

- Perform a comprehensive study of development adjacent to the park.

- Establish cooperative working relationships with local citizens, representatives, private- land owners, etc. to address disturbed land and viewshed issues.

Historic Landscape and Present Condition

Key resource management issues at Golden Spike National Historic Site are preserving the historic context including landforms and restoring and maintaining the natural environment. The relationship between rock units and erosional processes is dynamic. Changes in climate, especially precipitation, affect the entire system. Maintaining the balance between visitor access and use and preserving the historical and natural environment is a difficult but necessary task. The ~150- year written, oral and photographic record can be deciphered and correlated with sedimentation and erosion histories recorded along major streams such as Blue Creek. Correlating historic features captured in photographs such as the Union Pacific and Central Pacific parallel grades with parallel rock cuts, including the "false cut" just west of the Big Trestle/Big Fill area, trestle footings, major earth fills, stone wash culverts, former- trestle locations gives a clear indication of the evolution of the landscape since the railroad was completed. These grades, cuts, fills, and trestle footings represent nearly every variety of the heavy manual labor undertaken by the railroad workers except tunneling. Drill marks are still clearly visible in the numerous rock cuts. Railroad era borrow pits remain beside the grades (NPS website).

Inventory, Monitoring, and/or Research Needs for Historic Landscape and Present Condition

- Monitor and inventory human signatures in the park and other cultural resources.
- Study the role of enlarging fractures in the rock through solution weathering and freeze- thaw cycles.
- Study how different lithologies respond to weathering and erosion.
- Survey and map in detail the area surrounding the historic wash culvert present on the East Slope near the park, completed July 14, 1916.
- Develop an in- house plan to inventory, monitor, and protect significant historic resources from threats. Use assigned staff to oversee the implementation.
- Perform a detailed 3- dimensional cartographic survey of the area following appropriate standards and guidelines and include man- made features in the survey.
- Continue efforts to minimize the continuing erosion on the Union Pacific grade that is already severely eroded; temporarily mitigate the erosion by stabilizing the slope until more permanent measures are taken.

Paleontologic Potential

The desert landscape of Golden Spike contains more than a historic record of western expansion; it contains a record of prolific ancient life. Fossils at the park include algae, corals, snails, trilobites, clams, turtles, ammonites, oysters, and plants. It would be beneficial to protect and catalogue preserved specimens for scientific study, future generations, and increased visitor appreciation of the entire park.

Inventory, Monitoring, and/or Research Needs for Paleontologic Potential

- Perform a comprehensive study of the paleontologic resources at Golden Spike National Historic Site.
- Compile an inventory of all paleontologic specimens present in the park.
- Determine the locations of paleontologic specimens removed from the park as part of private collections.
- Draw visitor attention to the fossil resources at Golden Spike with graphics, brochures, and exhibits.

Faulting and Deformation Processes

The rock units at Golden Spike National Historic Site have undergone multiple phases of deformation resulting in folds, faults, joints, and other fractures, that create weaknesses in the rocks. Faults or fractures are zones where the rock has been cracked and even pulverized. Surface runoff loosens rock along faults and fractures that can eventually develop into a gulley.

Deformation is ongoing at Golden Spike and small scale fractures and joints are actively forming. Understanding the nature and location of these features allows predictions as to where weathering and erosion are likely to be concentrated - important information for resource management.

Inventory, Monitoring, and/or Research Needs for Faulting and Deformation Processes

- Conduct a detailed study of fractures, faults, and bedding in the area.
- Study the role of jointing and faulting (both strike- slip and thrust faulting) with landscape development and their interrelationship.
- Conduct an inventory of recent fault scarps in the area. These are commonly present in Quaternary surficial deposits.

Volcanic Potential

Recent volcanic deposits including tuff and basalt are present at Golden Spike. The volcanic features of Craters of the Moon lie to the north in southern Idaho (NPS website). The volcanic activity has been active at Craters of the Moon for the past 15,000 years and is probably responsible for the tuff layers present at Golden Spike. Because of its proximity to this volcanic center, it is possible that volcanic events could affect the Golden Spike area in the future.

Inventory, Monitoring, and/or Research Needs for Volcanic Potential

- Date applicable minerals to determine the age of lava flows.
- Determine the original volume of volcanic material in the park and the amount removed by erosion.
- Use resistivity to locate cavities in flows. These cavities could contain preserved animals, lava tubes, large vesicles, or other items.
- Conduct detailed mapping of volcanic terrain features in the volcanic field.

Wind Erosion and Deposition

In addition to water, wind is a major force that can redistribute soil and soil resources (e.g., litter, organic matter, and nutrients) within and among ecosystems. Erosion and deposition by wind are important at Golden Spike National Historic Site and can be accelerated by human activities.

Accelerated losses of soil and soil resources by erosion can indicate degradation of ecosystems because ecosystem health is dependent on the retention of these resources. Wind erosion and sediment transport may be strongly impacted by land- use practices outside the park. Human impacts within the park are associated primarily with off- trail hiking in high- use areas because park management practices limit or prohibit off- road vehicular travel. Accelerated soil erosion can be more extensive where livestock grazing or trailing is still permitted in surrounding areas. Grazing was permitted in the headquarters area for 73 years and led to extensive local erosion (NPS website).

Inventory, Monitoring, and/or Research Needs for Wind Erosion and Deposition

- Monitor movement of soil materials.
- Investigate the impacts to ecosystems from the aeolian transport of soil and soil materials.
- Investigate the variability of soil movement in relation to landscape configuration and characteristics.

General Geology

The geology at Golden Spike shaped the railroad grade and influenced the decisions made by engineers there. The tie between history and geology can enrich park decision making and the publics understanding of the opportunities and challenges that faced the railroad builders of the 19th century.

Inventory, Monitoring, and/or Research Needs for General Geology

- Identify unconformity- bounded stratigraphic packages in order to better define depositional systems in the past.
- Continue to implement geographic information systems (GIS) technology for interpretation, resource management, and maintenance through interpretive mapping, 3- D visualization, a virtual field trip, and surface rockfall hazard assessment.
- Develop more graphics and brochures emphasizing geology in cooperation with the Utah Geological Survey, Geologic Resources Division of the NPS, and NPS Cultural Resources targeted to the average enthusiast.

- Examine and date pack rat middens and examine the pollen record for recent climate history.
- Study, map, and date the Hansel Valley ash layer.
- Study and describe Pliocene upland valley blankets.
- Study ancient Lake Bonneville shorelines (including Provo, Bonneville, Stansbury, and Gilbert) in an attempt to find the Gilbert shoreline that has not yet been located within Golden Spike.

Cave Protection and Study

There is a cave present in the limestone units of the park. Cave systems are dynamic. Changes in water level, humidity, airflow, and light all have profound effects on the entire ecosystem. Water level and humidity affect any speleothems in the process of forming, drop by drop from mineral precipitation. The cave's location is not disclosed to the public or noted on the park map. Determining the balance between visitor access and cave preservation is a difficult task.

Inventory, Monitoring, and/or Research Needs for Cave Protection and Study

- Monitor and inventory human signatures in the cave, including any cultural and/or historical resources.
- Comprehensively study and monitor the atmospheric conditions and hydrology in the cave.
- Perform a detailed 3- dimensional cartographic survey that follows standards and guidelines of the cave interior including features (speleothems and speleogens).
- Study palynology and stratigraphy of sediments and cores.

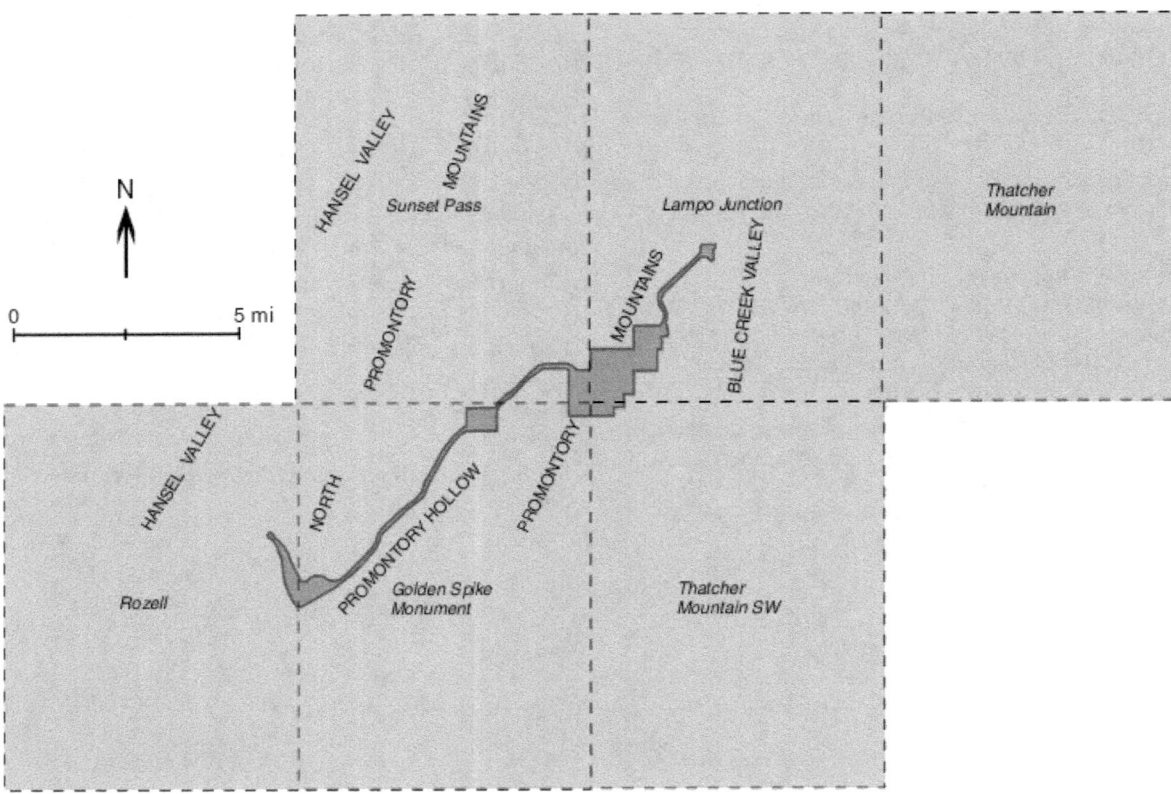

Figure 4. Map showing 7.5 minute quadrangles surrounding Golden Spike National Historic Site and prominent landforms including Hansel Valley, Blue Creek Valley, and the Sunset Pass area.

Geologic Features and Processes

This section provides descriptions of the most prominent and distinctive geologic features and processes in Golden Spike National Historic Site.

Chinaman's Arch

This unusual formation carved naturally from limestone is known as Chinaman's Arch (figure 5). It has become a memorial to the thousands of Chinese who helped build the transcontinental railroad from Sacramento, California. Because of labor shortages in California, Chinese were employed experimentally by the Central Pacific Railroad in 1865. Most were excellent workers and by 1868 over 10,000 Chinese people were working on the railroad.

Many of the Chinese remained with the Central Pacific after the completion of the railroad at Promontory, Utah. Travelers often noticed their clusters of tents along the rail route. Apparently, one such camp was near Promontory during the 1880's when this arch received its commemorative name.

Cut and Fills

Railroad engineers employed various methods to bring the new railroad route through the area within the required grade, a maximum of 2%. Cuts of various sizes exist at Golden Spike and are seen along the railroad grade. Conversely, many low areas had to be filled to conform to the grade requirement. When possible, material for the fills came from nearby cuts (figure 6).

The construction of railroad cuts was usually a difficult, time- consuming, and dangerous process. Teams of men and animals, even with the aid of black powder, could expect to spend weeks or months clearing out a rock cut of the size found on the Big Fill Walk. Cuts were created in a stair step fashion, enabling several crews at different levels to work on the cut simultaneously.

Big Fill

As late as December 1868, Central Pacific surveyors planned a railroad route that would require a 244 m- (800 ft) long tunnel be blasted through the eastern face of the Promontory Mountains. Central Pacific president Leland Stanford rejected this idea as too costly and time-consuming. After his veto, surveyors plotted a new route that would avoid tunneling. This new route required crossing Spring Creek ravine and in February 1869, work began on the Big Fill (figure 7).

The construction that followed took over 2 months of intense effort by 250 dumpcart teams and over 500 workers. Fill totaling over 10,000 cubic yards was hauled to the ravine and used to complete the 500- foot span of Spring Creek ravine at a depth of 70 feet.

The Big Fill has been in constant use since becoming part of the main line to Ogden, Utah. It was first a railroad route; then after removal of all rails in the area in 1942, it became an access road. It has been part of Golden Spike National Historic Site since 1965. The Big Fill has remained usable for over 130 years and is a lasting tribute to 1860's railroad engineering and construction.

Big Trestle

Just 46 m (150 ft) from the nearly completed Big Fill, construction began on the Union Pacific's Big Trestle on March 28, 1869. Since completion of the transcontinental railroad appeared imminent and the Union Pacific line was falling further behind the Central Pacific crew, it was decided that speed, not quality, was the overall construction goal. On May 5, just 3 days before the scheduled completion ceremony and only 36 days since building began, the last spike went into the 26 m (85 ft) high, 122 m (400 ft) long Big Trestle (figure 8).

The flimsy Big Trestle was never intended to be a permanent structure. As one newspaper reporter recorded, "It will shake the nerves of the stoutest hearts of railroad travelers when they see that a few feet of round timbers and 7- inch spikes are expected to uphold a train in motion" (figure 9). The trestle was abandoned in favor of the Big Fill when final control of the line passed to the Central Pacific. Within a few years, nothing remained of the Big Trestle except for Andrew J. Russell's photographs and the abutments that can still be seen today. This story lends credence to the dynamic geomorphological forces at work on the landscape of Golden Spike National Historic Site.

Lake Bonneville

The ancient Lake Bonneville covered the Golden Spike area from about 32,000 to 14,000 years ago. This lake, the precursor to the Great Salt and Utah lakes of today, was vast in size, about 523 km (325 mi) long and 217 km (135 mi) wide with a depth of over 305 m (1,000 ft). It is responsible for large deposits of lacustrine and other related Quaternary age deposits in the area during its 12,000- year regression from the area. Lacustrine marl silt, sand, and gravel cover the locale in bars, spits, and tombolos (see glossary) (Miller et al. 1991).

Lake Bonneville remained at constant depth for a prolonged period during its intermittent regression, leaving the shorelines with prominent horizontal benches and terraces on the adjacent hills and mountains.

Several of the most pronounced shorelines are called the Provo, Bonneville, Stansbury, and Gilbert shorelines at 1,594 to 1,600 m (5,230 to 5,250 ft), 1,487 to 1,478 m (4,880 to 4,850 ft), 1,329 to 1,364 m (4,360 to 4,475 ft), and 1,303 m (4,275 ft) in elevation, respectively (Miller and Schneyer 1994). For more information regarding Lake Bonneville, please refer to the following website: http://www.ugs.state.ut.us/online/PI-39/pi39pg01.htm

Older Structural Faults and Folds

Several large-scale faults and folds are present in the Golden Spike area. The Thatcher Mountain syncline is a north-trending feature that controls the distribution of bedrock units in the area in the southeastern portion of the Golden Spike area. The axial surface dips westward 40 to 50 degrees (Jordan et al. 1988).

The Blue Springs thrust fault is located southwest of Golden Spike National Historic Site. The fault passes from the southern Blue Springs Hills to Anderson Hill in the upper Blue Creek Valley with approximately 3,050 m (10,000 ft) of eastward translation (see figure 4) (Miller et al. 1991). The fault has a westward dip of about 35 degrees, and it places Oquirrh Formation rocks on top of the Thatcher Mountain syncline.

Another regional thrust fault, the Samaria thrust, parallels the Thatcher Mountain syncline and may be connected in origin to both the syncline and the Blue Springs thrust. This fault thrusts Pennsylvanian and Permian age rocks eastward relative to the Mississippian age and older rocks. The Samaria thrust fault is part of the Manning Canyon detachment system that underlies the Pennsylvanian and Permian bedrock north of Great Salt Lake (Jordan et al. 1988).

Basin and Range Features

High-angle normal faults cut all preexisting structures in the area surrounding Golden Spike National Historic Site.

Most of these faults trend north-south, but locally some are oriented east-west to the southeast of Golden Spike. These faults are usually steeply inclined with dips greater than 50 degrees. Many faults with inferred large offsets are covered with unconsolidated Quaternary age deposits, making documentation and measurement difficult. Areas underlain by thick sequences of Oquirrh Formation or Manning Canyon shale offer few stratigraphic markers to determine faulting. Engineer Mountain, the northern Promontory Mountains, and the central part of the Blue Springs Hills are probably cut by many unmapped, high-angle faults (Miller et al. 1991).

Offsets of several hundreds of feet are suggested by gravity anomalies, topographic breaks, and juxtaposition of rock units (Jordan et al. 1988). The Thiokol fault, located just northeast of Golden Spike, is a major north-striking fault that cuts the Blue Springs thrust fault. It dips steeply east and shows a large degree of stratigraphic separation down to the west, suggesting offsets as great as 450 m (1,500 ft) along its length (Miller et al. 1991). High angle faults bound the eastern and western sides of the North Promontory Block in the northwestern corner of the region. The western faults are grouped under the name North Promontory fault system, and the eastern faults are part of the development of the deep Miocene basin (Sand Hollow) (Miller and Schneyer 1994).

The North Promontory fault strikes north-northeast and is composed of two or more parallel fault strands. The faults dip moderately west at approximately 58 degrees. Segments of this fault are probably as young as Pleistocene in age (~16,000 years old) (Miller and Schneyer 1994). The faults accompanying development of the Sand Hollow basin on the eastern side of the North Promontory block all dip generally to the east. The sediments in the basin may be as much as 2,100 m (6,900 ft) thick (Miller and Schneyer 1994). For more information on the geologic structures and units featured on the digital geologic map of Golden Spike National Historic Site, please refer to the Windows helpfile GOSPGLG.hlp that accompanies the map.

Figure 5. Chinaman's Arch, a natural bridge carved from a limestone rock formation. Photograph courtesy of the National Park Service.

Figure 6. A cut along the railroad line grade through limestone. Photograph courtesy of the National Park Service.

Figure 7. The Big Fill as it appears today, still in use as a road at Golden Spike National Historic Site. Photograph courtesy of the National Park Service.

Figure 8. The Big Trestle at Promontory, Utah. Photograph from A.J. Russell. This and other Russell photographs are available at http://www.uprr.com/aboutup/photos/ajrussellstereo/r0528.shtml

Figure 9. A locomotive on the Big Trestle at Promontory, Utah. Photograph from A.J. Russell. This and other Russell photographs are available at http://www.uprr.com/aboutup/photos/ajrussellstereo/

Map Unit Properties

This section provides a description for and identifies many characteristics of the map units that appear on the digital geologic map of Golden Spike National Historic Site. The table is highly generalized and is provided for informational purposes only. Ground disturbing activities should not be permitted or denied on the basis of information contained in this table. More detailed unit descriptions can be found in the help files that accompany the digital geologic map or by contacting the NPS Geologic Resources Division.

Golden Spike National Historic Site is underlain almost entirely by Mesozoic rocks, with Tertiary rocks capping the high points. These rocks are strikingly visible due to regional erosion, uplift, and extension.

The Laketown Dolomite of Silurian age, is the oldest rock in the area. The Water Canyon, Beirdniau, Oquirrh, and Thatcher Mountain Formations; Gardison, Great Blue, and Deseret Limestones; and the Manning Canyon Shale were formed in a variety of depositional environments in the Devonian, Mississippian, Pennsylvanian, and Permian periods.

Extension characteristic of the Basin and Range province followed late Cretaceous to early Tertiary compressional Sevier–Laramide orogenic events. Tertiary basalts, tuff, loess and gravels and redeposited tuffs, interbedded with sandstone, shale, and marlstone of the Salt Lake Formation are the result of local tectonic activity.

Quaternary alluvium, colluvium, eolian sand, lacustrine sand and silt, and talus deposits overlie Tertiary and older underlying rock units.

During and after uplift, erosion carved the ravines, gullies, sweeping valleys, and channels present at Golden Spike today. Pleistocene glaciation and other geomorphological agents including streams and landslides have all left recent Quaternary age deposits on the landscape. The engineering of the railroad grade through the area introduced vast man- made fill deposits and cuts to the landscape.

The following pages present a tabular view of the stratigraphic column and an itemized list of features for each map unit. This sheet includes several properties specific to each unit present in the stratigraphic column including: map symbol, name, description, resistance to erosion, suitability for development, hazards, potential paleontologic resources, cultural and mineral resources, potential karst issues, recreational use potential, and global significance.

Map Unit Properties Table

Age	Unit Name (Symbol)	Features and Description	Erosion Resistance	Suitability for Development	Hazards	Potential Paleontologic Resources	Potential Cultural Resources	Mineral Specimens	Potential for Karst Issues	Mineral Resources	Habitat	Recreation Potential	Global Significance
QUATERNARY	Fill, alluvium, colluvium, lacustrine deposits, mass-movement, fan deposits and loess (Qf, Qal, Qae, Qai, Qarf, Qap, Qc, Qam, Qlso, Qlu, Qes, Qat/Qls, Qas, Qlu, Qmt, Qmm, Qms, Qao, Qli, Qlgs, Qlg, Qli, Qls, Qlm, Qla, Qat2, Qlf)	Assorted silts, sands, gravels and clays in streams, terraces, and lakes (Lake Bonneville shorelines and lake bottoms). Dark brown silts, sands and clays in flood plain deposits. Poorly sorted gravel, sand, silt and clay in alluvial fans. Some sand and silt are wind transported. Blocky, unsorted debris as talus fans and slides at the bases of slopes, and along former lake shores along with deposits of oolid sands.	Very low	Unconsolidated deposits could fail if water saturated and slope should be avoided for waste facilities and large structures, especially if slope is present	Slumps, slides, mass movement, flash flood washes, seismic activity and liquefaction a threat, gullying, debris flows and floods	Unknown	Valley fills on present land surface, ancient campsites?	None	None	Sand, gravel, clay, silt, boulders	Present day land surface, habitat for animals and plants	Good for all uses unless slope is present to create unstable, unconsolidated surface	Bonneville beach deposits record lake levels of glacial Lake Bonneville in regionally correlative terraces
QUATERNARY-TERTIARY	Alluvial Fan Deposits (QTaf3)	Unit is composed of moderately consolidated to caliche-cemented, poorly sorted deposits of boulders, cobbles, and pebbles forming highly dissected fans and terraces.	Very low to low	Poor cementation is likely to fail on slopes, high permeability for waste facility development	Slumps, slides and rockfall	Modern fossils possible	Ancient campsites, hunting areas	Caliche	None	Boulders, cobbles	Crevices and pores for burrows	Good for most recreation	Records rapid uplift
	Alluvium and Loess (QTal)	Unit is unconsolidated to cemented, white caliche-coated boulders, cobbles, and pebbles of quartzite, shale and siltstone near terrace crests. Underlain by red, well-bedded alluvium and fine sand and silt-sized loess. Thin to thick bedded.	Very low to low	Poor cementation is weak on slopes, high permeability for waste treatment	Rockfall, slides, slope creep	Modern fossils possible	Ancient campsites, hunting areas	Caliche	None	Boulders, cobbles, pebbles	Crevices and pores for burrows	Good for most light recreation	Records rapid uplift
TERTIARY	Eolian Loess and Alluvial Gravel (Tel)	Combined units of moderately consolidated red loess composed of locally thick accumulations of fine sand and silt size particles. Alluvium is well bedded with clasts of rounded to subangular quartzite, limestone, shale and siltstone	Low	Low consolidation makes unit vulnerable to rockfall and sliding, okay for most recreational use	Rockfall and slides, weak shales	Modern fossils possible, or derivations from earlier units	Ancient campsites, hunting areas	None	Some dissolution in limestone	Sand, silt	Crevices and pores for burrows	Picnic areas, campsites, trails	Records rapid uplift
	Basalt (Tb)	Dark gray to very dark gray, fine grained to very fine grained, crystal-rich olivine-pyroxene-plagioclase basalt. Classified as olivine tholeiite to basalt and consists of lava flows 3 to 12 m (10 to 40 ft) thick, each generally with a vesicular top and bottom. Flaggy to slaty appearance also present at some flow boundaries. Breccia present between some flows. Contains sparse phenocrysts of plagioclase, pyroxene, and quartz. Dated at about 3.5 Ma.	Moderate to high	Rough nature of surface makes it a poor choice for recreational development	Blockfall if undercut on slope, rough uneven surfaces for walking	None	Unknown	Oil and gas potential, phenocrysts plagioclase, pyroxene, quartz	None	Basalt rocks	Vesicles and crevices between flow provide burrow habitat	Rough trail base, unstable footing	3.5 Ma volcanic activity in the region, fresh surfaces
	Sedimentary Rocks and Tuff (Tt)	Unit is moderately consolidated, gray to brown air-fall tuff and tuffaceous rock redeposited in fluvial and lacustrine environments, and conglomerate and sandstone. Air-fall tuff is mainly glass shards, locally with feldspar and pumice. Redeposited tuff, generally sand and silt sized, contains varying amounts of lithic fragments. Unit is interbedded with sand, silt, and marl containing little tuff.	Low	Unit is suitable for most development, except in areas of pumice concentration (sharp surfaces)	Sharp volcanic glass surfaces, rockfall, slumps in lacustrine deposits	Modern fossils possible	Unknown	Pumice, tuff, shards, opals	None	None	Unknown	Sharp clasts should be avoided for trails	K-Ar dates of ~9-18 Ma, Records volcanic activity in the area
	Salt Lake Formation (Ts)	Unit is moderately consolidated, gray to brown air-fall tuffaceous rock redeposited in lacustrine environment. Redeposited tuff, generally sand-sized and silt-sized, contains varying amounts of lithic fragments, and is size-sorted and bedded; interbedded with sandstone, shale, and marlstone. Minimum thickness equals 100 m (330 ft).	Low	Low consolidation makes unit vulnerable to rockfall and sliding, okay for most recreational use	Rockfall, slides, slope creep	Modern fossils possible	Unknown	Tuff deposits	Some karst dissolution in marlstone	None	Unknown	Good for most light recreation	Radioactive dating, lacustrine deposits with volcanic record
PERMIAN — Thatcher Mountain Formation	Upper Member (Pt)	Unit is 1520 m (5000 ft) thick at type section. Upper member is thin-to thick-bedded, reddish-brown, fine- to coarse-grained sandstone, with local crossbeds and some limestone to dolomite interbeds. Bluish-gray nodular and anastamosing chert replaces some sandstone, interbedded with calcite and dolomite.	Moderate to high (increases with chert content)	Suitable for most development unless highly fractured	Rockfall, blockfall	Scant fossils in limestone layers	Chert nodules may have provided ancient tool material	None	Some in limestone and dolomite beds	Flagstone material	Dissolution pockets may provide nesting habitat	Climbing and most other recreation	Type section at Thatcher Mountain, paleocurrent in crossbeds
	Chert Member (Ptc)												
LOWER PERMIAN UPPER PENNSYLVANIAN — Oquirrh Formation	Thinly Bedded Member (Qot), Sandstone member (Posi), Silty limestone member (Posi), Bioturbated Limestone Member (PPNob), Limestone Member (PNot)	Unit is more than 3000 m (10000 ft) thick in the area. Unit is composed of coarse limestone, silty limestone and quart sandstone with medium to thick bedding. Calcisite beds with dark-brown chert lenses are common in the upper layers. Light-gray, medium-grained orthoquartzite and calcareous quartzite in beds more than 395 m (1300 ft) thick in sandstone member. Sandstone grades downward into light gray siltstone interbedded with brown limestone with some burrows and fossiliferous beds. Light-medium-gray, silty and sandy clastic limestone and brown, calcareous, very fine-grained quartz sandstone dominates lower beds. Bioturbated beds and laminated beds are interbedded on medium scale. Some chert nodules occur locally. Forms small cliffs.	High	Unit should be competent for most forms of development unless highly fractured or weathered	Rockfall hazard if rock is highly jointed or dissolved. Some shale layers may prove incompetent if highly weathered	Abundant early Pennsylvanian age fossils in conjunction with assorted tusulinids such as Millerella sp.	Chert nodules could have provided tool material	Fossils, banded layers	Karst potential exists for this unit	Building material, clean limestone	Vugs on cliff could provide nesting habitat, goat habitat	Good for most uses, weathered surfaces could prove hazardous for rock climbing	Unique, thick banded member prominent in region, Pennsylvanian age fossils

Age	Unit Name (Symbol)		Features and Description	Erosion Resistance	Suitability for Development	Hazards	Potential Paleontologic Resources	Potential Cultural Resources	Mineral Specimens	Potential for Karst Issues	Mineral Resources	Habitat	Recreation Potential	Global Significance
PENNSYLVANIAN	Manning Canyon Shale	Transitional Member (PNmct)	Transitional member is 150-210 m (490-680 ft) thick, whereas lower member is >915 m (3000 ft) thick. Unit forms layers of interbedded quartzite, siltstone, and medium-bedded fossiliferous limestone, transitional into the limestone member of the Oquirrh Formation. Units weather to tan and gray. Lower beds contain medium- to coarse-grained sandstone and bold, dark-brown quartzite interbedded with noon-resistant gray to black shale and minor fossiliferous limestone	Low to moderate	Rock weathers easily making it a poor foundation base for structures and most permanent development, especially if a slope is present	Severe slumping and sliding hazards exist for this unit on slopes and/or if water saturated	Brown shale contains fossil plants and abundant marine fossils	None	Fossils	Not enough carbonate present	Disseminated gold potential, clay products, lightweight aggregate, pyrophyllite	Burrowing material if highly weathered, forms gentle slopes in canyons for plant and animal habitat	Not stable enough for heavy use	Contains boundary between Upper Mississippian and Pennsylvanian ages near middle of unit
		Lower Member (PNMmc)												Unknown
MISSISSIPPIAN	Older Sedimentary Rocks (Pzs)		Unit contains beds of undifferentiated carbonate, sandstone, and shale typical of the region.	Moderate	Unit is suitable for most forms of development unless highly fractured	Rockfall, blockfall on slopes	Possible fossils in this unit	None	None	If carbonate content is high	None	Vugs on cliffs as nesting	Good for most recreation	Unknown
	Great Blue Limestone (Mgb)		Present only beneath the surface this unit is locally cherty, thick-bedded limestone containing abundant coral fossils.	Moderate to high	Suitable for most development unless significant dissolution or weathering has occurred. Dissolution can pose a problem with waste facilities.	Unit is only present in subsurface, some dissolution may produce caves and sinkholes	Late Mississippian age fossils	Chert nodules could have provided tool material	None	Karst potential exists for this unit	None documented	Caves and burrows	Unit is only present in subsurface	Type locality in the Oquirrh Mountains, thick carbonate deposit
	Humbug Formation and Deseret Limestone, Undivided (Mhd)		Only present in cross section of the area, these units are composed of brown sandy and silty limestone and calcareous siltstone with abundant fossils of corals, brachiopods.	Moderate (weathers as caves)	Dissolution can create conduits which pose a problem for waste facilities and severe dissolution can make construction on this unit risky	Unit is only present in subsurface, some dissolution may produce caves and sinkholes	Late Mississippian age brachiopods and corals, crinoid stems, cup corals and colonial corals	Native Americans may have used any caves present, chert masses may have been tool material	Speleothems (if caves present), fossils	Karst potential exists for this unit	Attractive building stone	Caves provide animal habitat, esp bats	Good for most recreation, caves, climbing	Distinct bands, hosts Timpanogos Cave system
	Gardison Limestone (Mg)		Only present in cross section of the area, unit is composed of dark-gray, thin-bedded limestone. Fossils are abundant.	High	Shaly partings can render the unit unstable for foundations and other permanent facilities	Unit is only present in subsurface, some dissolution may produce caves and sinkholes	Mississippian age fossils, some corals and brachiopods	Many chert nodules useful for ancient tools	Fossils	Some karst potential in carbonate beds	Locally uraniferous and phosphatic layers	Unknown for area	Unit is present in subsurface	Unit contains Mississippian fossils of Kinderhookian age
DEVONIAN	Beirdnau Formation (Db)		Present in cross section only, calcareous sandstone, dark dolomite and limestone dominate this unit.	Moderate to high	Unit is only in subsurface in park area, dissolution increased permeability may factor in to waste facility development.	Unit is only present in subsurface, some dissolution may produce caves and sinkholes	Fossils possible, noted elsewhere for this unit	None	None	Karst potential exists for this unit	None documented	Unknown for area	Unit is present in subsurface	Records ancient basin in Utah
	Hyrum Dolomite (Dh)		Unit is present in cross section only, but is composed of dolomite and limestone interbeds.	Moderate to high	Unit is only in subsurface in park area, dissolution increased permeability may factor in to waste facility development	Unit is only present in subsurface, some dissolution may produce caves and sinkholes	Fossils possible	None	None	Karst potential exists for this unit, esp in limestone beds	None documented	Unknown for area	Unit is present in subsurface	Records ancient basin in Utah
	Water Canyon Formation (Dwc)		Present in cross section only, unit contains conspicuously laminated light and dark-gray dolomite present in outcrop as bands.	High	Unit is only in subsurface in park area, dissolution increased permeability may factor in to waste facility development	Unit is only present in subsurface, some dissolution may produce caves and sinkholes	Fossils possible	None	Banded dolomite	Some karst potential exists for this unit	None documented	Unknown for area	Unit is present in subsurface	Records ancient basin in Utah
SILURIAN	Laketown Dolomite (Sl)		Unit is in cross section of the area only. Unit is composed of pale-gray to white dolomite with scant sandstone and limestone interbeds. Rather massive.	High	Unit is only in subsurface in park area, dissolution increased permeability may factor in to waste facility development	Unit is only present in subsurface, some dissolution may produce caves and sinkholes	Fossils possible	None	None	Karst potential exists for this unit	None documented	Unknown for area	Unit is present in subsurface	Records ancient basin in Utah

Geologic History

This section highlights the map units (i.e., rocks and unconsolidated deposits) that occur in Golden Spike National Historic Site and puts them in a geologic context in terms of the environment in which they were deposited and the timing of geologic events that created the present landscape.

Rocks in the Golden Spike National Historic Site area record a vast span of geologic history (figure 10). The oldest rocks provide a rare glimpse into the tectonic setting of the Proterozoic Era. The earliest event preserved and recorded by rocks exposed in the area was the deposition of the layers of sand and mud from nearby highlands that now form the uppermost part of the Big Cottonwood Formation (exposed in the Wasatch Range) of late Precambrian time. This formation is exposed in the deepest canyons cutting the Wasatch Mountains east of Golden Spike. The deposition was interrupted by a prolonged period of glaciation. The ancient glaciation was followed by local tectonic uplift and subsequent extreme erosion (Baker and Crittenden 1961).

Late Proterozoic rifting created a new continental margin along western North America. During the late Precambrian and through the Cambrian, thousands of feet of shallow- water marine sediments accumulated along a passive plate- tectonic margin on the western side of the Transcontinental Arch, an upland that stretched from present northern Minnesota southwestward across Nebraska, Colorado, and northwestern New Mexico (Speed 1983; Sloss 1988; Graham et al. 2002). The Golden Spike area was locatednear the western shoreline in this paleoenvironment (figure 11).

Throughout the Paleozoic Era, Europe, Africa, and South America were approaching North America as the two great landmasses, Laurasia and Gondwana, collided. The ancient continent of Gondwana included Australia, Antarctica, Africa, South America, and India south of the Ganges River, plus smaller islands. Laurasia, located in the northern hemisphere, is the hypothetical continent that contained the present northern continents (Graham et al. 2002).

The region again underwent uplift followed by severe erosion in the early Cambrian Period. The region subsided following the uplift, and an ancient sea advanced. The sea provided the depositional basin that captured vast amounts of sediments from the adjacent land mass. Sediments included the sand for the Tintic Quartzite and the mud for the Ophir Formation. As the basin subsided and the sea deepened, limy muds settled to the bottom, later lithifying into the Maxfield Limestone.

These units are all exposed in the Wasatch Mountains. This sequence of stratigraphic units records the deepening of the sea and advance of the shoreline. Late Precambrian shallow- water sediments thicken across

Utah from east to west, reaching a thickness of 3000-6000 m (10,000 to 20,000 ft) in western Utah (Hintze 1988; Graham et al. 2002).

Water covered virtually the entire state following the uplift and subsequent subsidence for a long stand of marine sediment deposition. The Equator ran northward through Utah, and limy muds accumulated under these warm- water conditions in much the same way as they do in the broad lime- mud shoal- bank area in the Bahaman Islands today (Hintze 1988).

Paleozoic rocks, specifically Silurian age rocks, are first to record the geologic history exposed at the surface in Golden Spike. Rocks of the Laketown Dolomite near Golden Spike document broad carbonate shelves evolving into open and restricted marine environments and later near- shore marine environments.

The first compressive pulses of the Antler Orogeny in the west and the Acadian Orogeny in the east (part of the Appalachian evolution's series of orogenic events) were felt in the Middle Devonian Period (about 401 Ma) as landmasses accreted onto both the western and eastern borders of North America. A subduction zone formed west of Utah, and lithospheric plates collided against one another bending, buckling, folding, and faulting into a north- south trending mountain range that stretched from Nevada to Canada. The Roberts Mountains Thrust marks the easternmost thrust sheets generated by the Antler Orogeny.

Great sheets of rock measuring tens to hundreds of kilometers in width and length were stacked on top of one another during orogenic events. The weight depresses the land in front of the thrust sheets, or *foreland*, and causes the foreland to subside into a *foreland basin*. As the highlands to the west thrust above sea level at the beginning of the Mississippian, warm marine water flooded the foreland basin and spread over eastern Utah and creating an extensive carbonate platform.

Fossils of animals that once lived in normal marine salinity including brachiopods, trilobites, corals, bryozoans, crinoids, fish, foraminifera, and conodonts (see Glossary)) are found in the thick Mississippian marine limestones. The sea became shallower during the regression that followed the Antler Orogeny, and habitats dwindled restricting animal life. Eastern Utah transitioned to a broad karst plain of shallow- marine sandstone and micrite (carbonate mudstone). The area was again exposed to subaerial erosion by the end of the Mississippian (Poole and Sandberg 1991; Graham et al. 2002).

Layers of carbonates, intermittently alternating with sandy sediments, accumulated in the area during Early Mississippian and much of Late Mississippian time. These were to become the Fitchville, Gardison, Deseret, and Humbug formations.

The sea became shallower during the regression that followed the Antler Orogeny, and the Kaskaskia Sequence (a prominent pile of cratonic deposition consisting of quartz sandstones, carbonates, and evaporites) came to an end. The shoreline again receded from the Transcontinental Arch; by early Pennsylvanian time, soils began forming in low lands and the higher areas experienced erosion. Coincident with Pennsylvanian tectonics (figure 12) was a global climate shift in the region of Utah from the warm humid environment of the Late Mississippian to a much more arid environment during the Early Pennsylvanian (Rueger 1996).

As the Ancestral Rocky Mountains formed, the Ouachita- Marathon thrustbelt, the Anadarko Basin, and other Permian basins developed to the south and the Oquirrh Basin subsided (Jordon and Douglas 1980; Peterson 1980; Kluth 1986; Gregson 1992). Vertical relief in some of these basins relative to sea level (i.e., the Oquirrh and Central basins) was greater than the emergent mountains. The Ancestral Rockies may have reached as much as 3,000 m (10,000 ft) of relief.

The thick sedimentary sequence of the Oquirrh Group east of the Golden Spike area represents the variety of shallow marine and arid near- shore environments present in the Oquirrh basin area throughout the Pennsylvanian. Included were eolian dunes, marine shelf, open coastal area, intermittent fluvial systems and channels, and calm storm buffered basins (Konopka 1982). The Oquirrh Basin, along with these other paleotectonic structures, probably reflects a regionally pervasive tectonic stress field. Precambrian structural weaknesses and the compressional stress field that evolved with the assembly of Pangaea (Tweto 1977; Kluth 1986; Ross and Ross 1986; Gregson 1992) likely controlled the basin and range structures.

Continuing from the Pennsylvanian and during the middle part of the deposition of the Permian Park City Formation, shallow, stagnant seas persisted over most of the region providing the arid, evaporitic conditions required for the deposition of phosphate and other salts (Baker and Crittenden 1961). The Permian Period appeared to be a time of dramatic environmental change across the globe. Wyoming and eastern Utah were oriented along a trend that placed the Permian equator on a southwest- northeast line through the area. An arid climate prevailed in this western part of the supercontinent Pangaea and resulted in restricted marine evaporitic conditions over much of the cratonic seaway

(Peterson 1980; Graham et al. 2002). These shallow seas filled the Oquirrh and Paradox basins today known for their incredible accumulations of sediments and salts.

Geologists have documented from deposits around the globe that the third and most extensive mass extinction in geologic time occurred at the close of the Permian. Although not as well known as the extinction that wiped out the dinosaurs at the end of the Mesozoic, the Permian extinction was much more widespread. The most recent hypothesis relating to this event suggests that a comet, about 6- 13 km (4 to 8 mi) in diameter, slammed into Earth (Becker et al. 2001).

Thousands of species of insects, reptiles, and amphibians perished on land. In the oceans, coral formations vanished as did snails, urchins, sea lilies, some fish, and the once- prolific trilobites. The extinction wiped out virtually 300 million years of life history. Five million years later, at the dawn of the Mesozoic Era, the oceans began a shift toward the chemistry of the modern oceans (Graham et al. 2002).

There are no Mesozoic rocks present in the walls east of and surrounding Golden Spike National Historic Site. They were eroded and removed from the area following uplift along regional faults. This missing rock record makes determining the paleoenvironment of the Mesozoic at Golden Spike difficult. Geologists refer to surrounding areas to determine the history in a regional context.

Periodic incursions from the north throughout the Triassic and Jurassic brought shallow seas flooding into Wyoming, Montana, and into a northeast- southwest trending trough on the Utah- Idaho border (figure 13). Volcanoes formed an arcuate north- south chain of mountains off the western coast in what is now central Nevada. To the south, the landmass that would become South America split away from the Texas coast. Africa and Great Britain rifted away from the present East Coast opening up the Atlantic Ocean. The Ouachita Mountains, formed when South America collided with North America, remained a significant highland, and rivers from this highland flowed to the northwest toward the Colorado Plateau. The Ancestral Rocky Mountains and the Monument Upwarp also remained topographically high during the Jurassic.

The Western Interior Basin was a broad, shallow sea on the southwest side of the North American craton during this time. The basin stretched northward from its southern margin in Arizona and New Mexico across the Canadian border. The basin was asymmetric with the rapidly subsiding Utah- Idaho trough along the west side and a more gently dipping shelf farther east.

At the beginning of the Middle Jurassic Period, the western Elko highlands emerged to the west of the Utah- Idaho trough. The highlands record an irregular, pulsed orogeny with continued compression along the western margin, at varied rates of motion (Peterson 1994). The sea lapped on to the continent from the north as plate tectonic activity increased to the west.

The next major tectonic event in the Golden Spike area has its origins in the Late Jurassic when a passive margin became a convergent continental boundary. The Sevier Orogeny began in the late Early Cretaceous (Albian age) and peaked in the Late Cretaceous. Slightly later, but overlapping in time (mid- Late Cretaceous to early Oligocene), the Laramide (Rocky Mountain) Orogeny formed the southern Rocky Mountains, Uinta Mountains, the San Rafael Swell, and other uplifted features to the east and south of Golden Spike. Both were in response to crustal shortening as the Farallon and North American plates collided. During the Sevier Orogeny in western Utah and southern Nevada, large thrust sheets moved eastward. Great compressional forces pushed these sheets of rock from west to east along thrust faults, first as thin slabs of sedimentary rocks, then as thick slabs with basement detachments. This formed overlapping columns of rock, and eventually enough rock was uplifted to create the Rocky Mountains (figure 14). This compression also resulted in the uplift of thousands of meters of sedimentary deposits that were buried in the basin that covered central Utah.

The Gulf of Mexico, separating North and South America, continued to rift open in the south. Marine water transgressed northward from the expanding Gulf of Mexico and southward from the Arctic into the roughly north- south trending trough east of the rising mountains.

The seas advanced, retreated, and advanced again many times during the Cretaceous until the most extensive interior seaway ever recorded drowned much of western North America. The Western Interior Seaway was an elongate basin that extended from today's Gulf of Mexico to the Arctic Ocean, a distance of about 4,827 km (3,000 mi) (Kauffman 1977). The width of the basin was 1,600 km (1,000 mi) from western Utah to western Iowa during periods of maximum transgression. The basin was relatively unrestricted at either terminus (Kauffman 1977).

The Late Cretaceous to early Tertiary rocks that crop out south of Golden Spike record Sevier orogenic deformation and its evolution into Laramide deformation (Goldstrand 1990). This deformation, contrasting with earlier Sevier deformation, involved thick, basement- cored uplifts along thrust faults that shallowed downward accompanied by extensive folding. The Sevier orogeny shoved relatively thin slabs of older, upper Precambrian and lower Paleozoic sedimentary rocks eastward over younger, upper Paleozoic and lower Mesozoic rocks.

For about 35 million years during the Laramide Orogeny, from roughly 70 Ma to 35 Ma, the collision of the tectonic plates transformed the extensive basin of the Cretaceous Interior Seaway into smaller interior basins bordered by rugged mountains (figure 15) (Graham et al.

2002). The crustal unrest of the Late Cretaceous Laramide orogeny culminated in the great dislocations along the Charleston thrust fault southeast of Great Salt Lake.

Following the extensive crustal thickening during the Laramide orogeny, melting of the lower crust during decompression gave rise to the volcanic activity of the Wasatch Igneous Belt. The emplacement of the belt was facilitated by mantle upwelling and underplating of a hot lower crust during the regional, Basin and Range crustal extension following decompression (Vogel et al. 1997). Near the end of the Laramide Orogeny in early mid- Tertiary time, igneous activity occurred across the southwest (Baars 2000; Fillmore 2000).

Laccoliths emplaced during this time provide some of the spectacular topography seen from national parks and monuments in Utah today, including the Henry, Abajo and La Sal Mountains (Graham et al. 2002). This onset of volcanic activity signaled the ultimate end of the Laramide Orogeny. The area's deformational regime changed once again from compressional to extensional and the southwestern margin of North America underwent extensional deformation. As crustal extension continued the surface developed into the basin- and- range topography of today in western Utah, Nevada, Arizona, and New Mexico.

Golden Spike is in the Basin and Range physiographic province and the Wasatch Front forms part of the eastern edge. The Wasatch Mountains are a narrow, uplifted fault- block range trending north- south from southern Idaho (Malad City, ID) to central Utah (Gunnison, UT), some 370 km (230 mi) (Swan et al. 1980). The Wasatch fault is defined for much of its extent by a zone of lesser faults and a well- marked fault scarp, the dramatically sharp Wasatch Front. The fault exhibits almost continuous geomorphic expression of late Quaternary uplift (Swan et al. 1980).

Uplift along the Wasatch ongoing today along the various segments of the Wasatch fault (figure 16). Though no significant seismic events have occurred in recorded history along the fault, geologists speculate an earthquake is possible at any moment. One of the largest of these segments located southeast of Great Salt Lake has a footwall of Great Blue limestone and a hanging wall of Manning Canyon shale. The top of the Great Blue limestone is displaced by this series of faults, from an elevation of about 2743 m (9,000 ft) to a position below the valley floor, making the total displacement more than 1219 m (4,000 ft) (Baker and Crittenden 1961). Estimates of average total throw across the fault zone vary from 2.6 to 4 km (1.6 to 2.5 miles) (Bruhn et al. 1987).

Fault- bounded valleys separating the uplifted mountain ranges are filled with a variety of sediments shed from the newly exposed highlands. In the Golden Spike area, during and after a period of intense regional erosion that probably occurred during much of the Eocene and early Oligocene, the conglomerates and reworked volcanics of the Tibble Fork Formation were deposited, possibly contemporaneous with volcanic rocks erupting in the Park City area to the northeast (Baker and Crittenden 1961).

The Quaternary Period is subdivided into two epochs: 1) the Pleistocene which ranges from about 1.6 Ma to 10,000 years before present (B.P.), and 2) the younger Holocene Epoch that extends from 10,000 years B.P. to the present. The Pleistocene Epoch, known as the Ice Age, is characterized by multiple episodes of continental and alpine glaciation. Great continental glaciers thousands of feet thick advanced and retreated over approximately 100,000- year cycles. Huge volumes of water were stored in the glaciers during glacial periods so that sea level dropped as much as 91 m (300 ft) (Fillmore 2000).

About 16,800 years ago, ancient Lake Bonneville covered an area larger than the Great Salt Lake. It was 305 m (1,000 ft) deep and the highest shoreline, called the Bonneville shoreline, was located around 1,565 m (5,135 ft) above sea- level. The Provo shoreline, at which level the water remained the longest, was a little over 1,463 m (4,800 ft) in elevation. Both are expressed by marked contours, parallel to the valley floor, along the foot of the Wasatch range (Baker and Crittenden 1961). In the foothills of the mountains in Utah and in the Salt Lake valley, benches of gravel and sand were deposited by Lake Bonneville. At the mouth of American Fork canyon,

southeast of Golden Spike near Timpanogos Cave National Monument, two large hills (about 30.5 m or 100 feet high) are formed by gravel deposited as the ancient American Fork River reached Lake Bonneville and formed a river delta.

Lake Bonneville once covered 51,800 square km (20,000 square mi) over Utah and parts of Nevada and Idaho. At Golden Spike Bonneville age lacustrine marl silt, sand, and gravel cover older sediments. Approximately 16,800 years ago, Lake Bonneville crested over a pass at Red Rocks (near Downey, Idaho) into southern Idaho. This breach sent a torrent of water out of Lake Bonneville and into the Snake River drainage. The water carved incredible deep valleys and left deposits of sand, gravel, and even boulders as it rushed along. The Bonneville flood lasted less than a year and lowered lake level by 122 m (400 ft). As Utah's climate became warmer and drier, Lake Bonneville slowly evaporated until the Great Salt Lake and Utah Lake were all that remained.

Geologically, the region around Golden Spike has changed little during the Holocene, the age of humans, with the exception of railroad development, blasting, and filling. Streams have modified the landscape since the end of the Pleistocene. Figure 17 summarizes the geologic history from the Proterozoic to the present at Golden Spike National Historic Site.

Eon	Era	Period	Epoch	Ma	Life Forms	N. American Tectonics
Phanerozoic (Phaneros = "evident"; zoic = "life")	Cenozoic	Quaternary	Recent, or Holocene		Age of Mammals — Modern man	Cascade volcanoes
			Pleistocene	0.01	Extinction of large mammals and birds	Worldwide glaciation
				1.8		
		Tertiary	Pliocene		Large carnivores	Uplift of Sierra Nevada
			Miocene	5.3	Whales and apes	Linking of N. & S. America
			Oligocene	23.0		Basin-and-Range Extension
				33.9		
			Eocene	55.8	Early primates	Laramide orogeny ends (West)
			Paleocene			
				65.5		
	Mesozoic	Cretaceous			Age of Dinosaurs — Mass extinctions	Laramide orogeny (West)
					Placental mammals	Sevier orogeny (West)
				145.5	Early flowering plants	Nevadan orogeny (West)
		Jurassic			First mammals	Elko orogeny (West)
				199.6	Flying reptiles	Breakup of Pangea begins
		Triassic			First dinosaurs	Sonoma orogeny (West)
				251		
	Paleozoic	Permian			Age of Amphibians — Mass extinctions	Super continent Pangea intact
					Coal-forming forests diminish	Ouachita orogeny (South)
						Alleghenian (Appalachian) orogeny (East)
				299		Ancestral Rocky Mts. (West)
		Pennsylvanian			Coal-forming swamps	
				318.1	Sharks abundant	
		Mississippian			Variety of insects	
					First amphibians	
				359.2	First reptiles	Antler orogeny (West)
		Devonian			Mass extinctions	
					Fishes — First forests (evergreens)	Acadian orogeny (East-NE)
				416		
		Silurian			First land plants	
				443.7	Mass extinctions	
		Ordovician			First primitive fish	
					Trilobite maximum	Taconic orogeny (NE)
					Rise of corals	
				488.3		
		Cambrian			Marine Invertebrates — Early shelled organisms	Avalonian orogeny (NE)
						Extensive oceans cover most of N.America
				542		
	Proterozoic ("Early life")	Precambrian			1st multicelled organisms	Formation of early supercontinent
						First iron deposits
					Jellyfish fossil (670Ma)	Abundant carbonate rocks
				2500		
Archean ("Ancient")					Early bacteria & algae	
				~3600		Oldest known Earth rocks (~3.93 billion years ago)
Hadean ("Beneath the Earth")					Origin of life?	Oldest moon rocks (4-4.6 billion years ago)
						Earth's crust being formed
				4600		Formation of the Earth

Figure 10. Geologic time scale; adapted from the U.S. Geological Survey. Red lines indicate major unconformities between eras. Included are major events in life history and tectonic events occurring on the North American continent. Absolute ages shown are in millions of years.

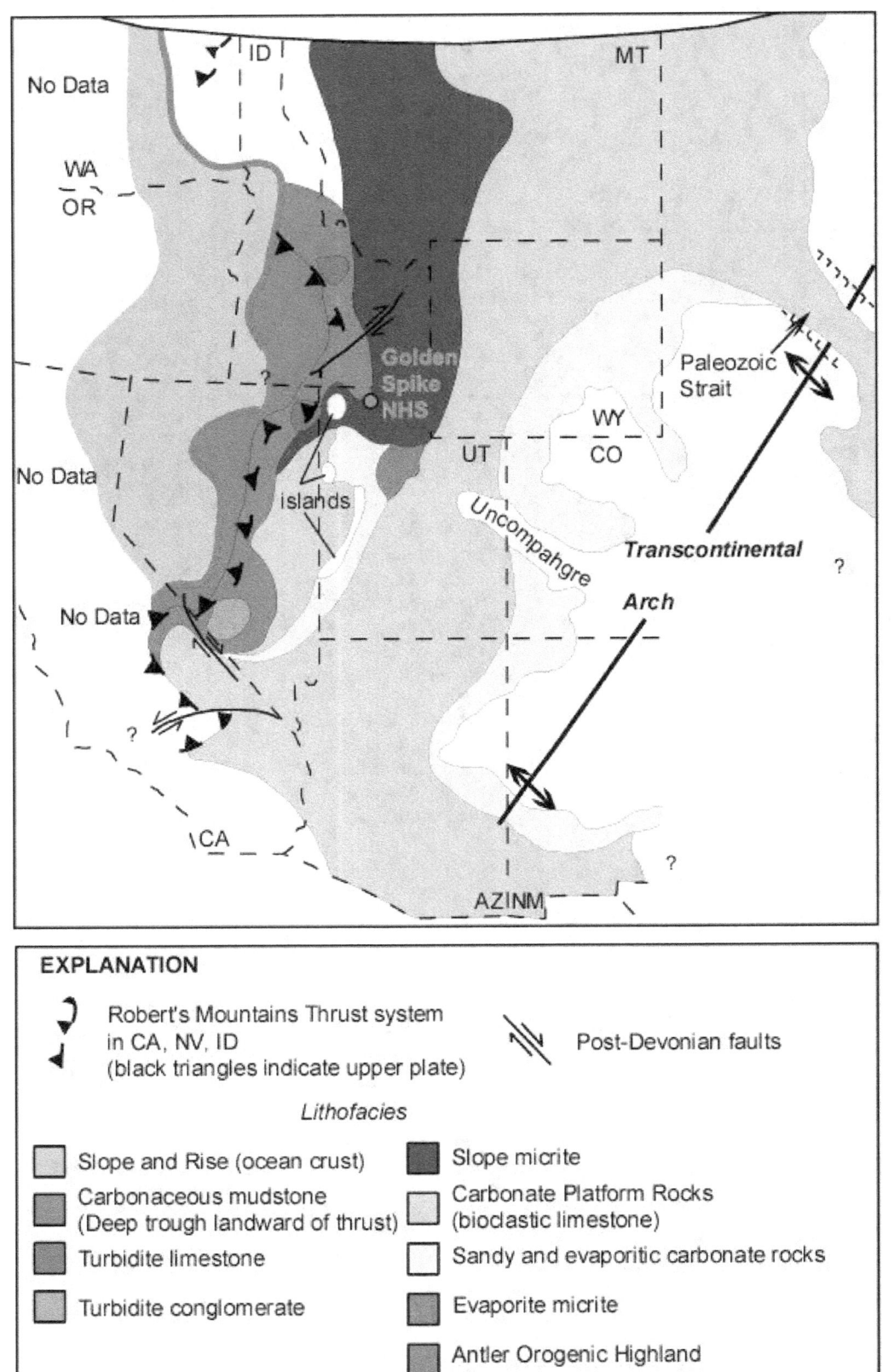

EXPLANATION

⌇ Robert's Mountains Thrust system in CA, NV, ID (black triangles indicate upper plate)

⫽ Post-Devonian faults

Lithofacies

◻ Slope and Rise (ocean crust)

◻ Carbonaceous mudstone (Deep trough landward of thrust)

◻ Turbidite limestone

◻ Turbidite conglomerate

◻ Slope micrite

◻ Carbonate Platform Rocks (bioclastic limestone)

◻ Sandy and evaporitic carbonate rocks

◻ Evaporite micrite

◻ Antler Orogenic Highland

Figure 11. Paleogeographic map of Early Mississippian age. Note the location of Golden Spike in relation to Transcontinental Arch.

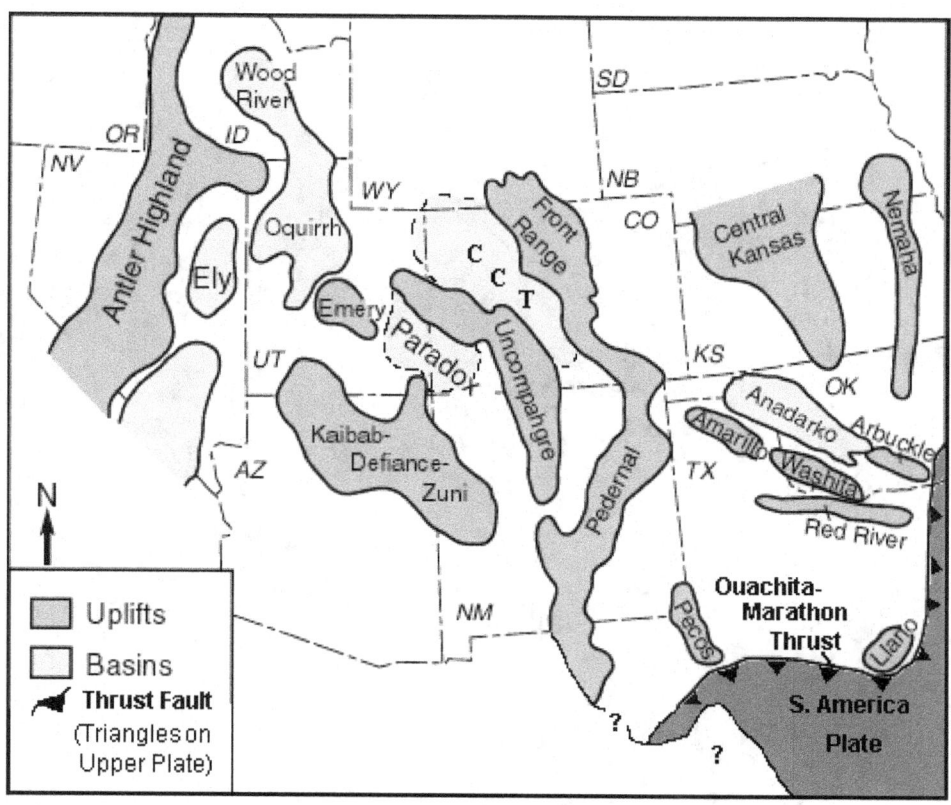

Figure 12. Major uplifts and basins present during the Pennsylvanian age in the southwestern United States. Sediment eroded from the uplifts was deposited in adjacent basins. Modified from Rigby (1977).

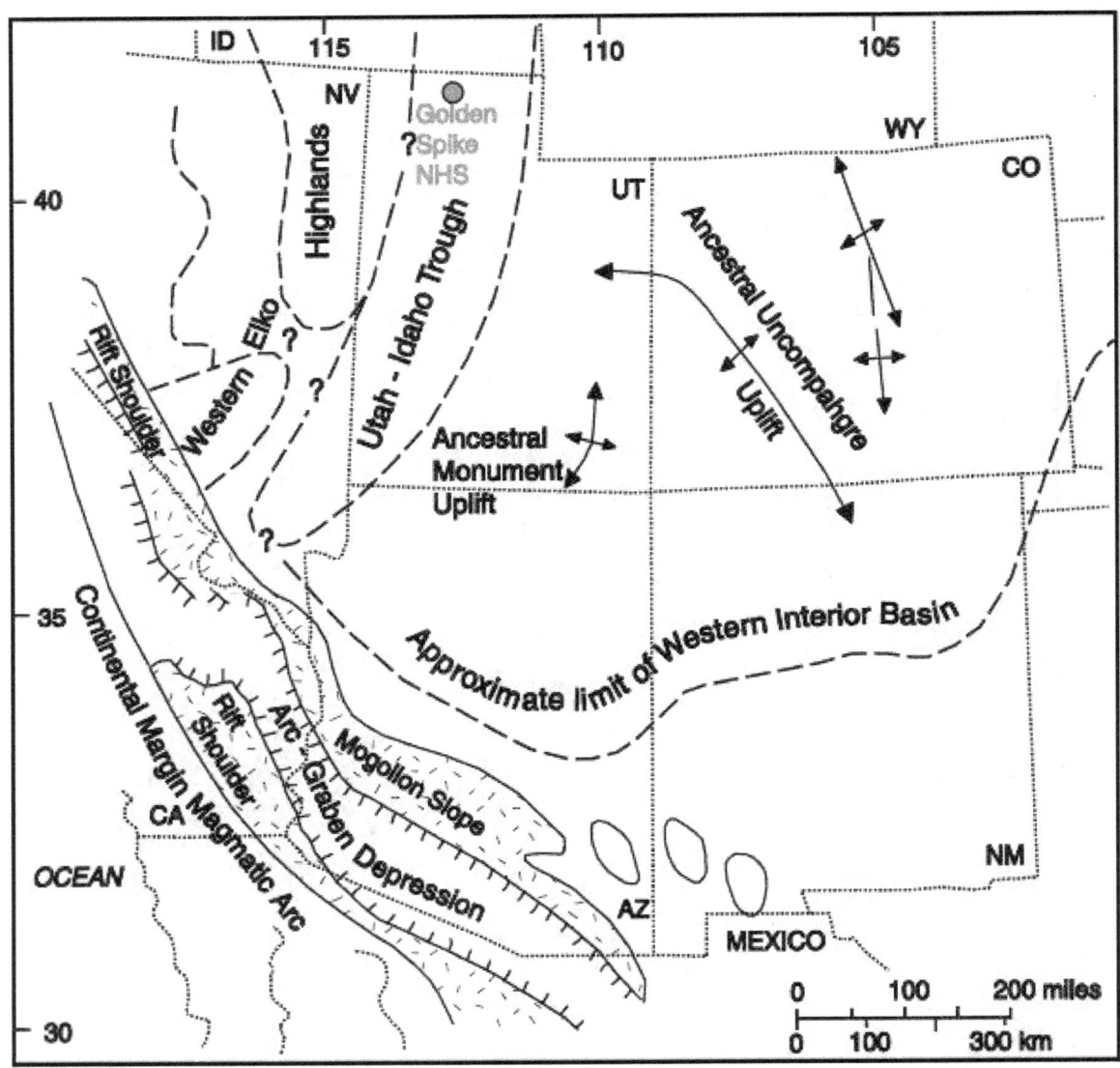

Figure 13. Jurassic structural elements affecting sedimentation in the western U.S. The arc-graben depression probably did not exist in Late Jurassic time. Eastern Elko highlands rose out of the Utah-Idaho trough in latest Middle and Late Jurassic time. Modified from Peterson (1994).

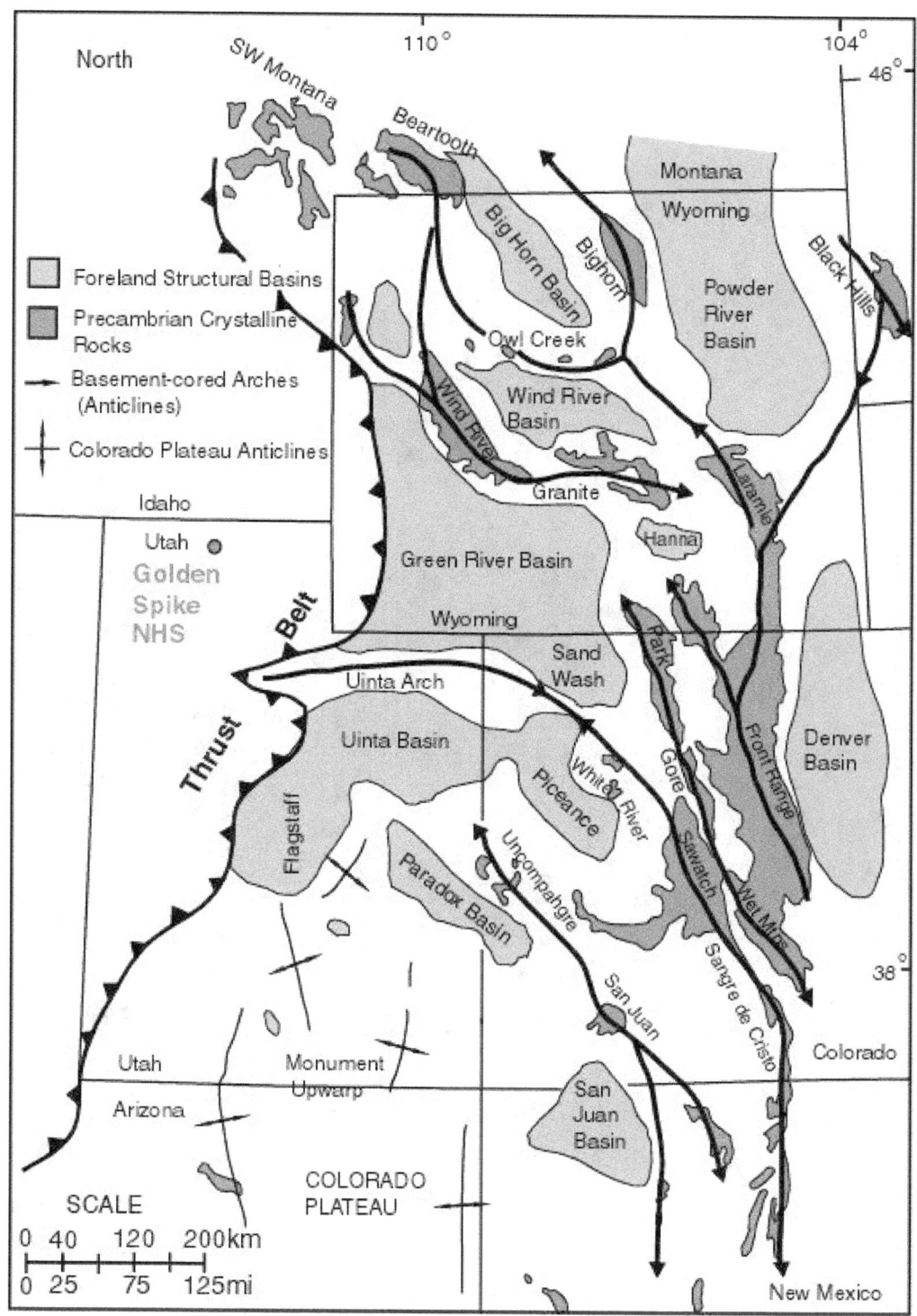

Figure 14. Location of Golden Spike National Historic Site on a tectonic map showing Laramide-age structures in the Western U.S. The map illustrates the anastamosing nature of the basement-cored arches (regional-scale anticlines) and the spatial relationships with the adjacent thrust belt, Colorado Plateau, and North American craton. The 'Thrust Belt' marks the eastern extent of the Sevier Orogeny. Note the location of Golden Spike, west of the Sevier Thrust Belt. Adapted from Gregson and Chure (2000).

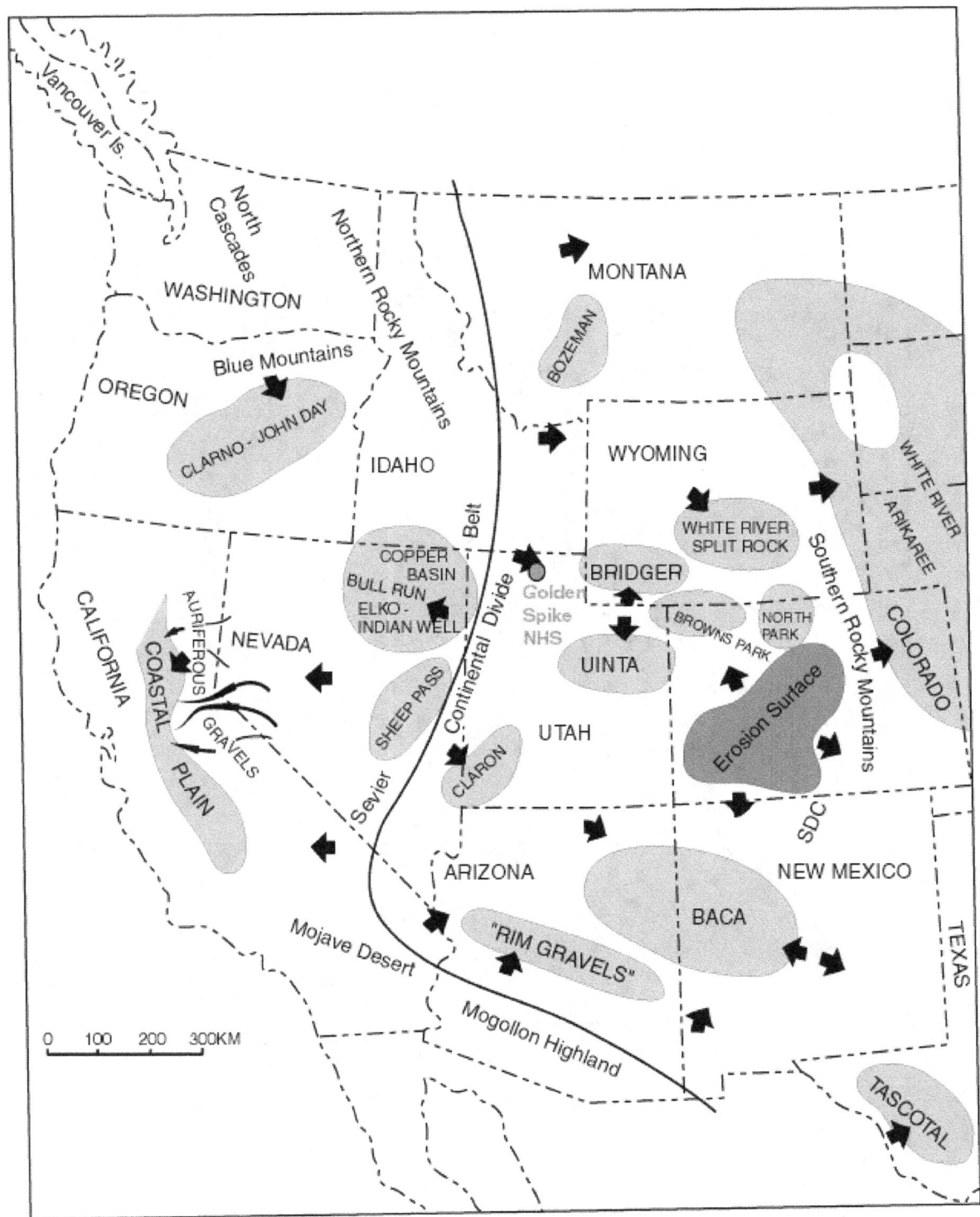

Figure 15. Early post-Laramide map showing the probable location of the continental divide, major depositional basins, erosional features, and stream systems in the western US. Light gray areas denote basins, dark gray areas indicate highlands, and arrows indicate probable directions of sediment transport into the basins and away from the continental divide. SDC = Sangre de Cristo Mountains; SJ = San Juan Mountains. Modified from Christiansen et al. (1994).

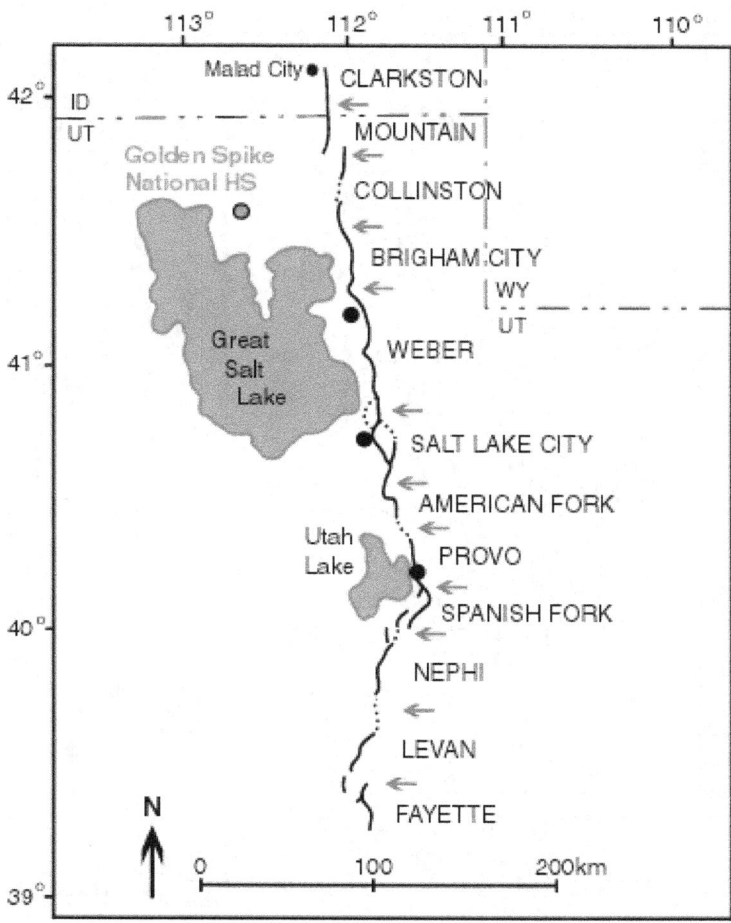

Figure 16. Segments of the Wasatch fault as identified by Machette (1987). Boundaries are placed at offsets of discontinuities in the trend of the fault and are marked by red arrows. Adapted from Hintze (1988).

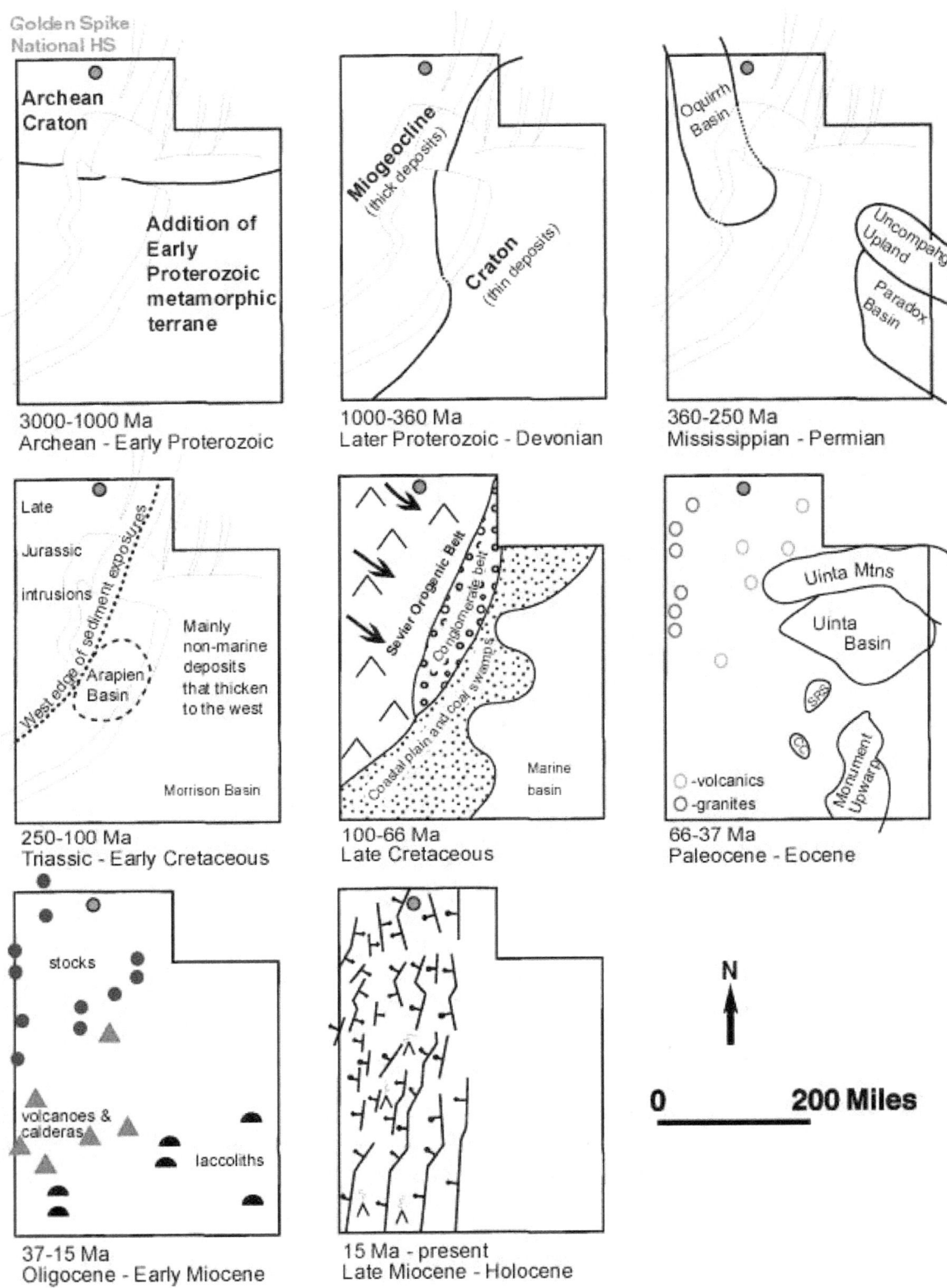

Figure 17. Generalized graphic overview of geologic evolution of Utah from the Archean Eon to the Holocene Epoch. Adapted from Hintze (1988).

Glossary

This glossary contains brief definitions of technical geologic terms used in this report. Not all geologic terms used are referenced. For more detailed definitions or to find terms not listed here please visit http://wrgis.wr.usgs.gov/docs/parks/misc/glossarya.html.

active margin. A continental margin where significant volcanic and earthquake activity occurs; commonly a convergent plate margin.

alluvial fan. A fan-shaped deposit of sediment that accumulates where a high gradient stream flows out of a mountain front into an area of lesser gradient such as a valley.

alluvium. Stream-deposited sediment that is generally rounded, sorted, and stratified.

angular unconformity. An unconformity where the strata above and below are oriented differently; generally caused by structural deformation and erosion prior to deposition of the upper bed.

aquifer. Rock or sediment that are sufficiently porous, permeable, and saturated to be useful as a source of water.

ash (volcanic). Fine pyroclastic material ejected from a volcano (also see tuff).

basement. The undifferentiated rocks, commonly igneous and metamorphic, that underlie the rocks of interest.

basin (structural). A doubly-plunging syncline in which rocks dip inward from all sides (also see dome).

basin (sedimentary). Any depression, from continental to local scales, into which sediments are deposited.

bed. The smallest sedimentary strata unit, commonly ranging in thickness from one centimeter to a meter or two and distinguishable from beds above.

bedding. Depositional layering or stratification of sediments.

bedrock geology. The geology of underlying solid rock as it would appear with the sediment, soil, and vegetative cover stripped away.

block (fault). A crustal unit bounded by faults, either completely or in part.

chemical weathering. The dissolution or chemical breakdown of minerals at Earth's surface via reaction with water, air, or dissolved substances.

conglomerate. A coarse-grained sedimentary rock with clasts larger than 2 mm in a fine-grained matrix.

continental drift. The concept that continents have shifted in position over Earth (see and use 'plate tectonics').

convergent boundary. A plate boundary where two tectonic plates are moving together (i.e., a zone of subduction or obduction).

cordillera. A Spanish term for an extensive mountain range that is used in North America to refer to all of the western mountain ranges of the continent.

cross section. A graphical interpretation of geology, structure, and/or stratigraphy in the third (vertical) dimension based on mapped and measured geological extents and attitudes depicted in an oriented vertical plane.

crust. The outermost compositional shell of Earth, 10-40 km (6-25 mi) thick, consisting predominantly of relatively low-density silicate minerals (also see oceanic crust and continental crust).

crystalline. Describes the structure of a regular, orderly, repeating geometric arrangement of atoms

debris flow. A rapid and often sudden flow or slide of rock and soil material involving a wide range of types and sizes.

deformation. A general term for the process of faulting, folding, shearing, extension, or compression of rocks as a result of various Earth forces.

delta. A sediment wedge deposited at a stream's mouth where it flows into a lake or sea.

dip. The angle between a structural surface and a horizontal reference plane measured normal to their line of intersection.

divergent boundary. A tectonic plate boundary where the plates are moving apart (e.g., a spreading ridge or continental rift zone).

drainage basin. The total area from which a stream system receives or drains precipitation runoff.

exfoliation. The breakup, spalling, peeling, flaking, etc. of layers or concentric sheets from an exposed rock mass due to differential stresses resulting from thermal changes or pressure unloading.

extrusive. Of or pertaining to the eruption of igneous material onto the surface of Earth.

fault. A subplanar break in rock along which relative movement occurs between the two sides.

formation. Fundamental rock-stratigraphic unit that is mappable and lithologically distinct from adjoining strata and has definable upper and lower contacts.

fracture. Irregular breakage of a mineral; also any break in a rock (e.g., crack, joint, fault)

geology. The study of Earth including its origin, history, physical processes, components, and morphology.

graben. A down-dropped structural block bounded by steeply-dipping, normal faults (also see horst).

horst. An uplifted structural block bounded by high-angle normal faults.

igneous. Refers to a rock or mineral that originated from molten material; one of the three main classes or rocks: igneous, metamorphic, and sedimentary.

intrusion. A body of igneous rock that invades older rock. The invading rock may be a plastic solid or magma that pushes its way into the older rock.

joint. A semi-planar break in rock without relative movement of rocks on either side of the fracture surface.

laccolith. A tack head- to arcuate- shaped, concordant pluton that domed or up- arched the overlying country rocks.

lacustrine. Pertaining to, produced by, or inhabiting a lake or lakes.

landslide. Any process or landform resulting from rapid mass movement under relatively dry conditions.

lava. Magma that has been extruded out onto Earth's surface, both molten and solidified.

limbs. The two sides of a structural fold on either side of its hingeline.

lithification. The conversion of sediment into solid rock.

lithology. The description of a rock or rock unit, especially the texture, composition, and structure of sedimentary rocks.

lithosphere. The relatively rigid outmost shell of Earth's structure, 50 to 100 km (31 to 62 mi) thick, that encompasses the crust and uppermost mantle.

loess. Silt- sized sediment deposited by wind, generally of glacial origin.

magma. Molten rock generated within Earth that is the parent of igneous rocks.

mantle. The zone of Earth's interior between crust and core.

mechanical weathering. The physical breakup of rocks without change in composition (syn: physical weathering).

member. A lithostratigraphic unit with definable contacts that subdivides a formation.

metamorphic. Pertaining to the process of metamorphism or to its results.

normal fault. A normal fault is defined as a surface where the hanging wall (the block above the fault surface) appears to have moved downward relative to the footwall (the block below the fault surface).

orogeny. A mountain- building event, particularly a well- recognized event in the geological past (e.g. the Laramide orogeny).

outcrop. Any part of a rock mass or formation that is exposed or "crops out" at Earth's surface.

paleontology. The study of the life and chronology of Earth's geologic past based on the phylogeny of fossil organisms.

Pangaea. A theoretical, single supercontinent that existed during the Permian and Triassic Periods (also see Laurasia and Gondwana).

plateau. A broad, flat- topped topographic high of great extent and elevation above the surrounding plains, canyons, or valleys (both land and marine landforms).

plate tectonics. The theory that the lithosphere is broken up into a series of rigid plates that move over Earth's surface above a more fluid aesthenosphere.

progradation. The seaward building of land area due to sedimentary deposition.

regression. A long- term seaward retreat of the shoreline or relative fall of sea level.

reverse fault. A contractional, high angle (>45°), dip- slip fault in which the hanging wall moves up relative to the footwall (also see thrust fault).

rock. A solid, cohesive aggregate of one or more minerals or mineraloids.

scarp. A steep cliff or topographic step resulting from vertical displacement on a fault or by mass movement.

slope. The inclined surface of any geomorphic feature or rational measurement thereof (syn: gradient).

slump. A generally large, coherent mass movement with a concave- up failure surface and subsequent backward rotation relative to the slope.

soil. Surface accumulation of weathered rock and organic matter capable of supporting plant growth and often overlying the parent rock from which it formed.

strata. Tabular or sheetlike masses or distinct layers (e.g., of rock).

stratigraphy. The geologic study of the origin, occurrence, distribution, classification, correlation, age, etc. of rock layers, especially sedimentary rocks.

strike. The compass direction of the line of intersection that an inclined surface makes with a horizontal plane.

strike-slip fault. A fault with measurable offset where the relative movement is parallel to the strike of the fault.

subduction zone. A convergent plate boundary where oceanic lithosphere descends beneath a continental or oceanic plate and is carried down into the mantle.

subsidence. The gradual sinking or depression of part of Earth's surface.

syncline. Down folded strata (concave upward)where the stratigraphically younger rocks are in the core and become progressively older outward

talus. Rock fragments, usually coarse and angular, lying at the base of a cliff or steep slope from which they have been derived.

tectonic. Relating to large- scale movement and deformation of Earth's crust.

tectonics. The geological study of the broad structural architecture and deformational processes of the lithosphere and aesthenosphere (also see structural geology).

terraces (stream). Step- like benches surrounding the present floodplain of a stream due to dissection of previous flood plain(s), stream bed(s), and/or valley floor(s).

terrestrial. Relating to Earth or Earth's dry land.

thrust fault. A contractional, dip- slip fault with a shallowly dipping fault surface (<45°) where the hanging wall moves up and over relative to the footwall.

topography. The general morphology of Earth's surface including relief and location of natural and anthropogenic features.

trace (fault). The exposed intersection of a fault with Earth's surface.

trace fossils. Sedimentary structures, such as tracks, trails, burrows, etc., that preserve evidence of organisms' life activities, rather than the organisms themselves.

unconformity. A surface within sedimentary strata that marks a prolonged period of nondeposition or erosion.

uplift. A structurally high area in the crust, produced by movement that raises the rocks.

weathering. The set of physical, chemical, and biological processes by which rock is broken down in place.

References

This section provides a listing of references cited in this report. It also contains general references that may be of use to resource managers. A more complete geologic bibliography is available and can be obtained through the NPS Geologic Resources Division.

Adams, O.C. 1962. *Geology of the Summer Ranch and North Promontory Mountains.*

Baars, D.L. 2000. *The Colorado Plateau.* Albuquerque, NM: University of New Mexico Press.

Baker, A.A., and M.D. Crittenden, Jr. 1961. *Geology of the Timpanogos Cave Quadrangle, Utah,* U.S Geological Survey: Quadrangle Map - GQ- 0132.

Blake, D., year unknown, http://www.media.utah.edu/UHE/g/GOLDENSPIKE. html (accessed April 11, 2004)

Bruhn, R.L., P.R. Gibler, W.T. Parry. 1987. Rupture characteristics of normal faults, An example from the Wasatch fault zone, Utah. *Journal of the Geological Society of London* 28: 337- 353.

Christiansen, E. II, B.J. Kowallis, M.D. Barton. 1994. Temporal and spatial distribution of volcanic ash in Mesozoic sedimentary rocks of the Western Interior, an alternative record of Mesozoic magmatism. In *Mesozoic Systems of the Rocky Mountain Region, USA,* eds. M.V. Caputo, J.A. Peterson, K.J. Franczyk, 73- 94. Denver, CO: Rocky Mountain Section, SEPM.

Crittenden, M.D., Jr. 1988. *Bedrock geologic map of the Promontory Mountains, Box Elder County, Utah.* U.S. Geological Survey, Open- File Report - OF 88- 0646.

De Courten, F. 1994. *Shadows of time – the geology of Bryce Canyon National Park.* Bryce Canyon, UT: Bryce Canyon Natural History Association.

Fillmore, R. 2000. *The Geology of the parks, monuments and wildlands of Southern Utah.* University of Utah Press.

Goldstrand, P.M. 1990. *Stratigraphy and paleogeography of Late Cretaceous and Early Tertiary rocks of southwest Utah,* Utah Geological and Mineral Survey, Miscellaneous Publication - MP90- 2.

Graham, J.P., T.L. Thornberry, S.A. O'Meara. 2002, Unpublished. *Geologic resources inventory for Mesa Verde National Park.* National Park Service, Inventory and Monitoring Program.

Gregson, J.D., D.J. Chure. 2000. Geology and paleontology of Dinosaur National Monument, Utah-Colorado. In *Geology of Utah's Parks and Monuments,* eds. D.A. Sprinkel, T.C. Chidsey, Jr., P.B. Anderson. Utah Geological Association publication 28.

Gwynn, J.W. 2002. The railroads proximate to Great Salt Lake, Utah. In *Great Salt Lake; an overview of change,* ed. Gwynn, J.W., 273- 281.

Hintze, L.F.. 1988. *Geologic history of Utah.* Brigham Young University Geologic Studies, Special Publications 7.

Hood, J.W. 1972. *Hydrologic reconnaissance of the Promontory Mountains area, Box Elder County, Utah.* State of Utah, Department of Natural Resources Technical Publication 38.

Jordan, T.E., R.C. Douglass. 1980. Paleogeography and structural development of the late Paleozoic to early Permian Oquirrh Basin, northwestern Utah. In *Paleozoic paleogeography of the west- central United States,* eds. T.D. Fouch, E.R. Magathan, 217- 238. SEPM (Society for Sedimentary Geology).

Jordan, T.E., M.D. Crittenden Jr., R.W. Allmendinger, D.M. Miller. 1988. *Geologic map of the Thatcher Mountain Quadrangle, Box Elder County, Utah.* U.S. Geological Survey, for Utah Geological and Mineral Survey, Utah Department of Natural Resources, MAP 109.

Kauffman, E.G. 1977. Geological and biological overview, Western Interior Cretaceous Basin. *Mountain Geologist* 14: 75- 99.

Ketterson, F.A., Jr. 1969. Golden Spike National Historic Site: Development of an historical reconstruction. Utah *Historical Quarterly* 37: 58- 68.

Kluth, C.F. 1986. Plate tectonics of the ancestral Rocky Mountains. In *Paleotectonics and sedimentation in the Rocky Mountain region,* ed. J. A. Peterson, 353- 369. AAPG Memoir 41.

Konopka, E.H., R.H. Dott Jr. 1982. *Stratigraphy and sedimentology, lower part of the Butterfield Peaks Formation (Middle Pennsylvanian), Oquirrh Group, at Mt. Timpanogos, Utah.* Utah Geological Association Publication 10: 215- 234.

Kraus, G. 1969. Chinese laborers and the construction of the Central Pacific. *Utah Historical Quarterly* 37: 41- 57.

Lohman, S.W. 1981. *The geologic story of Colorado National Monument.* U.S. Geological Survey - Bulletin 1508.

Machette, M.N., W.R. Lund. 1987. Late Quaternary history of the American Fork segment of the Wasatch fault zone, Utah. *Geological Society of America – Abstracts with program* 19: 317.

Mann, D.H. 1969. The Undriving of the Golden Spike. *Utah Historical Quarterly* 37: 124- 134.

Michel, L.V. 1986. *The Overthrust Belt in front of the Uinta Mountains*. Utah.

Miller, D.M., M.D. Crittenden Jr., T.E. Jordan. 1991. *Geologic Map of the Lampo Junction Quadrangle, Box Elder County, Utah*. U.S. Geological Survey, for Utah Geological and Mineral Survey, Utah Department of Natural Resources, MAP 136.

Miller, D.M., J.D. Schneyer. 1994. *Geologic Map of the Sunset Pass Quadrangle, Box Elder County, Utah* U.S. Geological Survey, Utah Geological and Mineral Survey, Utah Department of Natural Resources, MAP 154.

Miller, D.M. 2000. *Geologic Map of the Rozel Quadrangle, Box Elder County, Utah*. U.S. Geological Survey, Administrative report to the National Park Service, Map Unpublished.

Peterson, F. 1994. Sand dunes, sabkhas, stream, and shallow seas: Jurassic paleogeography in the southern part of the Western Interior Basin. In *Mesozoic Systems of the Rocky Mountain Region, USA*, eds. M.V. Caputo, J.A. Peterson, K.J. Franczyk, 233- 272. Denver, CO: Rocky Mountain Section, SEPM.

Peterson, J.A. 1980 Permian paleogeography and sedimentary provinces, west central United States. In *Paleozoic Paleogeography of the West- Central United States*, eds. T.D. Fouch, E.R. Magathan, 271- 292. Denver, CO: Rocky Mountain Section, SEPM.

Poole, F.G., C.A. Sandberg, C. A. 1991. Mississippian paleogeography and conodont biostratigraphy of the western United States. In *Paleozoic Paleogeography of the Western United States – II*, eds. Cooper, John D., Calvin H. Stevens, 107- 136. Society of Economic Paleontologists and Mineralogists (SEPM), Pacific Section.

Prucha, C.P. 1988. *Lineament study from satellite imagery of the Promontory Mountains in Utah.*

Prucha, C.P., D.W. Stearns, T.H.L. Williams. 1988. Comparison of Landsat TM and stereo SPOT imagery for structural geology interpretation in the Promontory Mountains, Utah. *Proceedings of the Thematic Conference on Geologic Remote Sensing* 6: p.449.

Ross, C.A., J.R.P. Ross. 1986. Paleozoic paleotectonics and sedimentation in Arizona and New Mexico. In *Paleotectonics and Sedimentation in the Rocky Mountain Region*, ed. Peterson, J.A., 653- 668. American Association of Petroleum Geologists Memoir 41.

Rueger, B. F. 1996. *Palynology and its relationship to climatically induced depositional cycles in the Middle Pennsylvanian (Desmoinesian) Paradox Formation of Southeastern Utah*. U.S. Geological Survey Bulletin 2000- K, 4 plates.

Sloss, L.L. 1988. Tectonic evolution of the craton in Phanerozoic time. In *Sedimentary Cover – North American Craton*, ed. Sloss, L.L., 25- 52. Geological Society of America, Geology of North America D- 2.

Speed, R.C. 1983. Evolution of the sialic margin in the central western United States. In *Studies in continental margin geology*, eds. Watkins, S., C.L. Drake, 457- 468. American Association of Petroleum Geologists Memoir 34.

Swan, F.H., III, D.P. Schwartz, L.S. Cluff. 1980. Recurrence of moderate to large magnitude earthquakes produced by surface faulting on the Wasatch fault zone, Utah. *Bulletin Seismological Society of America* 70: 1431- 1432.

Tweto, O. 1977. *Nomenclature of Precambrian rocks in Colorado*. U.S. Geological Survey Bulletin 1422- D.

Vogel, T.A., F.W. Cambray, L. Feher, K.N. Constenius. 1997. Petrochemistry and emplacement history of the Wasatch igneous belt, central Wasatch Mountains, Utah. *Geological Society of America – Abstracts with Programs* 29 (6): A- 282.

Appendix A: Geologic Map Graphic

The following page provides a preview or "snapshot" of the geologic map for Golden Spike National Historic Site. For a poster size PDF of this map or for digital geologic map data, please see the included CD or visit the GRE publications webpage: http://www2.nature.nps.gov/geology/inventory/gre_publications.cfm

Geologic Map of Golden Spike NHS and Vicinity

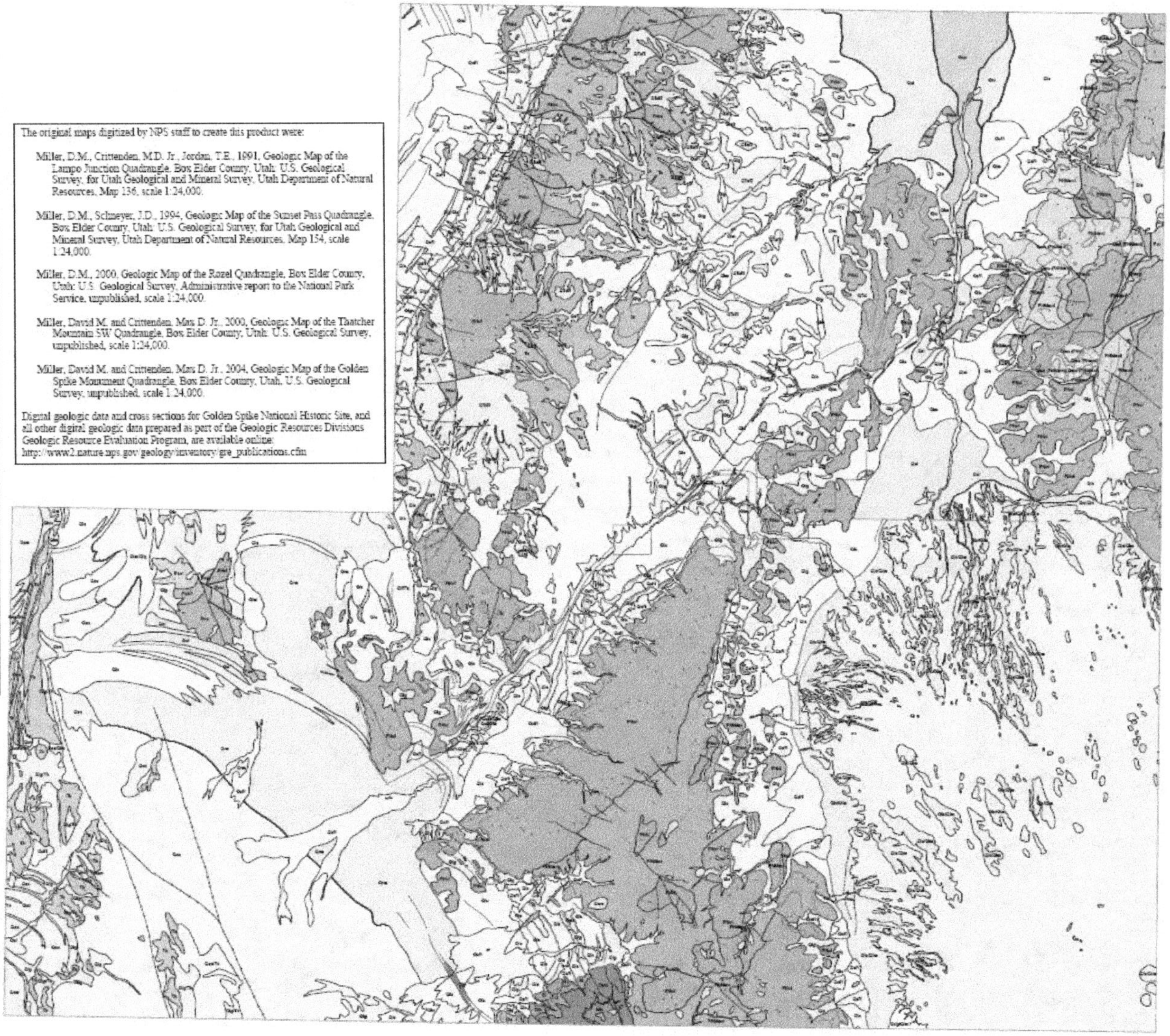

Geologic Units

- Qf - Fill
- Qal - Alluvium
- Qae - Alluvial and eolian deposits, undivided
- Qai - Alluvial silt
- Qaf1 - Alluvial fan deposits
- Qap - Alluvial-plain deposits
- Qam - Spring muck
- Qam - Alluvial mud
- Qes - Eolian sand
- Qmc1 - Mass-movement colluvium
- Qmt - Mass-movement talus
- Qai/Qls - Alluvial silt overlying Lacustrine sand
- Qlsc - Lacustrine cool sand
- Qmc2 - Mass-movement colluvium
- Qla - Lacustrine and alluvial deposits, undivided
- Qms - Mass-movement slides
- Qas - Alluvial sand and silt
- Qrm - Reworked marl
- Qls - Lacustrine sand
- Qls/Qlm - Lacustrine sand overlying Lacustrine marl
- Qdg/Qlm - Deltaic gravel and sand overlying Lacustrine marl
- Qlg - Lacustrine gravel
- Qlgs - Lacustrine gravel and sand
- Qlm - Lacustrine marl
- Qaf2 - Alluvial fan deposits
- Qlf - Lacustrine fine-grained sediment
- Qa - Andesite
- QTaf3 - Alluvial fan deposits
- QTal - Alluvium and loess, undivided
- Tb - Basalt
- Tel - Eolian loess and alluvial gravel
- Ts - Sedimentary rocks and tuff
- Pot - Oquirrh Formation, Thinly bedded member
- Pob - Oquirrh Formation, Bioturbated limestone member
- Pos - Oquirrh Formation, Sandstone member
- Pocl - Oquirrh Formation, Clastic limestone member
- Posl - Oquirrh Formation, Silty limestone member
- PPNo - Oquirrh Formation, undifferentiated
- PPNob - Oquirrh Formation, Bioturbated limestone member
- PNol - Oquirrh Formation, Limestone member
- PNmct - Manning Canyon Shale, Transitional member
- PMMmc - Manning Canyon Shale
- PMMmcl - Manning Canyon Shale, Lower member
- Mgb - Great Blue Limestone
- Mh - Humbug Formation
- Mdg - Deseret Limestone and Gardison Limestone, undivided
- Dwc - Water Canyon Formation
- Sl - Laketown Dolomite
- Ofh - Fish Haven Dolomite
- Oe - Eureka Quartzite

Golden Spike NHS

Attitude Measurements and Symbology

- anticline symbol
- fold plunge arrow head
- strike and dip of beds
- strike and dip of beds
- strike and dip of foliation
- strike and dip of foliation and bedding
- strike and dip of overturned beds
- strike and dip of overturned beds
- strike of vertical beds
- syncline symbol

Age-Date Localities

- Age-Date Localities

Paleoshorelines

- Paleoshorelines

Landslides

- landslide

Geologic Folds

- known or certain

Marker Beds

- Marker Beds

Geologic Faults

- known or certain
- approximate
- concealed
- concealed, queried
- inferred
- inferred, queried

Geologic Contacts

- known or certain
- approximate
- concealed
- gradational
- inferred
- quadrangle boundary

The original maps digitized by NPS staff to create this product were:

Miller, D.M., Crittenden, M.D. Jr., Jordan, T.E., 1991, Geologic Map of the Lampo Junction Quadrangle, Box Elder County, Utah: U.S. Geological Survey, for Utah Geological and Mineral Survey, Utah Department of Natural Resources, Map 136, scale 1:24,000.

Miller, D.M., Schneyer, J.D., 1994, Geologic Map of the Sunset Pass Quadrangle, Box Elder County, Utah: U.S. Geological Survey, for Utah Geological and Mineral Survey, Utah Department of Natural Resources, Map 154, scale 1:24,000.

Miller, D.M., 2000, Geologic Map of the Rozel Quadrangle, Box Elder County, Utah: U.S. Geological Survey, Administrative report to the National Park Service, unpublished, scale 1:24,000.

Miller, David M. and Crittenden, Max D. Jr., 2000, Geologic Map of the Thatcher Mountain SW Quadrangle, Box Elder County, Utah: U.S. Geological Survey, unpublished, scale 1:24,000.

Miller, David M. and Crittenden, Max D. Jr., 2004, Geologic Map of the Golden Spike Monument Quadrangle, Box Elder County, Utah, U.S. Geological Survey, unpublished, scale 1:24,000.

Digital geologic data and cross sections for Golden Spike National Historic Site, and all other digital geologic data prepared as part of the Geologic Resources Divisions Geologic Resource Evaluation Program, are available online: http://www2.nature.nps.gov/geology/inventory/gre_publications.cfm

0 1 2 4 Miles

0 1.5 3 6 Kilometers

N

Produced by Geologic Resources Division

June 2006

Appendix B: Scoping Summary

The following excerpts are from the GRE scoping summary for Golden Spike National Historic Site. The scoping meeting occurred on June 15- 16, 1999; therefore, the contact information and Web addresses referred to herein may be outdated. Please contact to the Geologic Resources Division for current information.

An inventory workshop was held at Golden Spike National Historic Site (NHS) on June 14- 15, 1999, to view and discuss the site's geologic resources, to address the status of geologic mapping for compiling both paper and digital maps, and to assess resource management issues and needs. Cooperators from the NPS Geologic Resources Division (GRD), Natural Resources Information Division (NRID), Columbia Cascades Support Office (CCSO), Golden Spike NHS (interpretation, resource management and superintendent), U.S. Geological Survey (USGS), and Utah Geological Survey (UGS) were present for the 2-day workshop.

Day one involved a field trip led by USGS Geologist Dave Miller who has done extensive geologic mapping and research in the Golden Spike NHS area. *Day two* involved a scoping session to present overviews of the NPS Inventory and Monitoring (I&M) program, the Geologic Resources Division, and the ongoing Geologic Resource Evaluation (GRE). Round table discussions involving geologic issues for Golden Spike NHS included interpretation, paleontological and cave and karst resources, the status of cooperative geologic mapping efforts, sources of available natural resource data, geologic hazards and other management issues, unique geologic features, potential future research topics, and action items generated from this meeting. Brief summaries of each are presented below.

Interpretation

The GRE aims to help promote geologic resource interpretation within the parks, and GRD has staff and technology to assist in preparation of useful materials including developing site bulletins and resource management proposal (RMP) statements appropriate to promoting geology. Jim Wood (GRD) and Melanie Moreno (USGS- Menlo Park, CA) have worked with several other NPS units in developing web- based geology interpretation themes and are a source of assistance if the park desires.

One of the major topics of discussion centered around the development of a publication describing the geology of Golden Spike to be available to visitors, perhaps something as simple as a brochure that could be printed with little cost. Mark Milligan (UGS Extension Services) offered to assist park staff in preparation of such a document, and it is hoped that such a joint NPS- UGS publication can be produced for GOSP. GOSP, GRD, and UGS staff will follow- up.

Paleontological and Speleological Resources

Paleontological and speleological natural resources were briefly discussed, and the following items were pointed out as being noteworthy for Golden Spike:

- Fossil corals and crinoids in the Paleozoic Oquirrh Formation,
- Ostracodes in White Marl (latest Pleistocene, from Lake Bonneville deposits), and
- Pack rat middens at an undisclosed cave location within the NHS.

Vince Santucci (NPS- GRD Paleontologist) is assembling an NPS service- wide paleontological database and should be consulted about any information he may have for GOSP.

Status of Geologic Mapping Efforts for Golden Spike

Dave Miller (USGS- Western Region in Menlo Park, CA) has done extensive geologic mapping for the USGS in cooperation with the UGS in the Golden Spike area. He has worked on several quadrangles and has compiled a *1:100,000* scale geologic map that encompasses the following 7.5' quadrangles:

- Lampo Junction: M- 136; *Geologic Map of the Lampo Junction quadrangle, Box Elder County, Utah* by D.M. Miller, M.D. Crittenden Jr., and T.E. Jordan, 17 p., 2 plates, 1991, $5.00. Publisher: USGS,
- Sunset Pass: M- 154; *Geologic Map of the Sunset Pass quadrangle, Box Elder County, Utah* by D.M. Miller and J.D. Schneyer, 14 p., 2 plates, 1994, $6.00. Publisher: USGS,
- Rozel, and
- Golden Spike Monument.

Lampo Junction and Sunset Pass are available from the UGS bookstore in Salt Lake City and contain paper maps and write- ups on the geology of the quadrangles. Adrienne Anderson thought that the Lampo Junction quadrangle needed more work regarding fills along the railroad (Blue Creek?).

The Rozel and Golden Spike Monument quadrangles have fieldwork completed but need to be compiled for final publication. The Thatcher Mountain Southwest quadrangle still needs some fieldwork. Dave estimates that it would take him a few months to deliver finished products if he were assigned to work on these maps.

The UGS will be publishing the 30x60 Tremonton quadrangle at *1:100,000* scale, but this scale would be too broad for park use. Miller's existing work at *1:24,000* scale is most desirable. His services need to be obtained to complete these three unfinished quadrangles.

GOSP Superintendent Bruce Powell volunteered to write a friendly letter to the USGS requesting Miller's services for this NPS project.

Other Sources of Natural Resources Data for Golden Spike

Adrienne Anderson (NPS- Intermountain Region; cultural resources) presented maps of the cultural areas within GOSP. She also drew attention to the layouts that Dave Hammond has prepared and the 100,000- scale compilation that Dave Miller has put together based upon the five quadrangles previously mentioned.

Dave Miller has supplied some additional bibliographic sources to add to the master bibliography for GOSP, based on material taken from his published Sunset Pass and Lampo Junction quadrangle. These need to be added to the IM database.

Consult with Larry Martin about the NPS- WRD "Drinking Water Source Protection Plan" 4- 99.

Geologic Hazards

There are numerous issues related to geologic hazards in and around Golden Spike NHS. Below is a brief list supplied by Dave Miller from his Sunset Pass quadrangle summary report. Please consult this publication directly if you desire more information.

Floods. Floods have potential for creating hazards in much of the Sunset Pass quadrangle. A potential exists for debris flows and floods on alluvial fans. Several Holocene alluvial fans mapped along both sides of the North Promontory Mountains have been active since the deposition of Bonneville lacustrine deposits; all are probable sites for future alluviation, including deposition during floods. Narrow canyons upslope from the fans are also likely sites for powerful floods and debris flows.

Gullying. Gullying has occurred in many areas underlain by unconsolidated to moderately consolidated materials. The uplands undergoing intensive agriculture east of the North Promontory Mountains show especially pronounced gullying. The fine- grained Miocene, Pliocene, and Quaternary materials in the Sunset Pass quadrangle are highly susceptible to the erosion that results from destroying natural ground cover.

Earthquakes. Northern Utah is part of a seismic belt characterized by numerous small- magnitude events and by potential for infrequent major events.
The region from Hansel Valley east to the Wasatch Mountains has experienced considerable historic seismic activity including magnitude 6 and larger events in Hansel Valley in 1909 and 1934.

No fault scarps or faults cutting upper Pleistocene deposits were discovered during field investigations. The youngest faults cut the oldest alluvial fan deposits of Pliocene and Pleistocene age but not upper Pleistocene

materials, and, therefore, probably are no younger than middle Pleistocene in age. However, several Quaternary and historic surface ruptures have been documented within a short distance of the Sunset Pass area, and Holocene alluvium or talus may have covered similar young scarps in the quadrangle. During 1934, a magnitude 6.6 earthquake occurred in Hansel Valley, and surface rupture from this event is documented about 8 km (5 mi) west of the Sunset Pass quadrangle. The western flank of the North Promontory Mountains has a particularly abrupt topographic expression. Jordan (1985) and Robison and McCalpin (1987) mapped normal faults cutting Pleistocene alluvial fan deposits in one area and Lake Bonneville deposits in another north of the Sunset Pass quadrangle along the mountain front.

The regional history of seismic activity and evidence for Quaternary faults in Hansel Valley raise the possibility of moderate to large earthquakes in the Sunset Pass quadrangle. The Wasatch fault zone and related faults 50- km (30 mi) to the east project westward at moderate angles, presenting a potential for a major seismic event that could strongly shake the Sunset Pass area. In addition to hazards from ground shaking and surface rupture, lateral spreads and liquefaction could result from an earthquake.

Landslides. Landslides are present as a few isolated slides within lacustrine deposits and Miocene strata. The slumps within lacustrine materials in the east- central part of the quadrangle involve thick lacustrine gravel deposits that probably were built northward by shoreline processes, overlapping finer grained sediments. These features create steep, unstable slopes where slides are likely to occur.

Also mentioned during the meeting was the possibility for volcanism.

Potential Research Topics for Golden Spike National Historic Site

- A list of potential research topics and future needs includes the following:
- Pack rat midden studies for recent climate history for pollen record.
- GOSP is an excellent candidate for studies of the interaction among climate change, land- use history, and landscape processes including erosion and deposition. The ~150- year photographic, written, and oral record can be deciphered along with sedimentation and erosion histories recorded along major streams such as Blue Creek.
- Study the deposition behind culverts and filled grades for their historic flood history. Compare the findings with the historic record of climate. Use this information to evaluate the stability of fragile culverts and trestles.

Disturbed Lands

The following were classified as disturbed lands and include sites to restore:

- Borrow pits for gravel.
- Sites to restore:
- Lands where impacts of grazing are visible,
- Private land gravel pit that is an eyesore,
- The Union Pacific grade where it has been eroded; minimize erosion for now,
- Wash Culvert dated 7- 14- 1916; Area where we talked about Dave Steensen (NPS- GRD Disturbed Lands coordinator) assisting GOSP staff, and
- Gravel operation on Adams Ranch that is an eyesore.

Unique Geologic Features

The Golden Spike area has some unique geologic features including the following:

- Chinaman's Arch,
- Flood deposits behind railroad embankments,
- Hansel Valley ash layer,
- Pliocene upland valley blankets,
- Lake level strand lines from the Provo, Bonneville, and Stansbury shorelines (the Gilbert shoreline, however, is not exposed),
- Views of the Great Salt Lake,
- The cave in the park (but its location is not disclosed to the public or noted on park maps), and
- Pack rat middens.

List of Scoping Meeting attendees with contact information

NAME	AFFILIATION	PHONE	E- MAIL
Bruce Heise	NPS, Geologic Resources Division	(303) 969- 2017	Bruce_Heise@nps.gov
Joe Gregson	NPS, Natural Resources Information Division	(970) 225- 3559	Joe_Gregson@nps.gov
Tim Connors	NPS, Geologic Resources Division	(303) 969- 2093	Tim_Connors@nps.gov
Marsha Davis	NPS, Columbia Cascades Support Office	(206) 220- 4262	Marsha_Davis@nps.gov
Dave Miller	USGS	(650) 329- 4923	Dmiller@usgs.gov
Mark Milligan	UGS	(801) 537- 3326	Nrugs.mmilliga@ut.state.us
Grant Willis	UGS	(801) 537- 3355	Nrugs.gwillis@state.ut.us
Bruce Powell	NPS, GOSP	(435) 471- 2209 ext. 12	Bruce_M._Powell@nps.gov
Rick Wilson	NPS, GOSP	(435) 471- 2209 ext. 19	Rick_Wilson@nps.gov
Adrienne Anderson	IMDE- CNR, Archaeologist	(303) 969- 2846	Adrienne_Anderson@nps.gov

Golden Spike National Historic Site
Geologic Resource Evaluation Report

Natural Resource Report NPS/NRPC/GRD/NRR—2006/010
NPS D-215, July 2006

National Park Service
Director • Fran P. Mainella

Natural Resource Stewardship and Science
Associate Director • Michael A. Soukup

Natural Resource Program Center
The Natural Resource Program Center (NRPC) is the core of the NPS Natural Resource Stewardship and Science Directorate. The Center Director is located in Fort Collins, with staff located principally in Lakewood and Fort Collins, Colorado and in Washington, D.C. The NRPC has five divisions: Air Resources Division, Biological Resource Management Division, Environmental Quality Division, Geologic Resources Division, and Water Resources Division. NRPC also includes three offices: The Office of Education and Outreach, the Office of Inventory, Monitoring and Evaluation, and the Office of Natural Resource Information Systems. In addition, Natural Resource Web Management and Partnership Coordination are cross-cutting disciplines under the Center Director. The multidisciplinary staff of NRPC is dedicated to resolving park resource management challenges originating in and outside units of the national park system.

Geologic Resources Division
Chief • David B. Shaver
Planning Evaluation and Permits Branch Chief • Carol McCoy

Credits
Author • Trista Thornberry-Ehrlich
Editing • Sid Covington and Melanie Ransmeier
Digital Map Production • Heather Stanton
Map Layout Design • Melanie Ransmeier